TRAVE
THEAT

C000009566

Ek performance and Traverse Theatre Company

What We Know

By Pamela Carter

cast in order of appearance

Lucy	Kate Dickie
Jo	Paul Thomas Hickey
Teenager	Lorn Macdonald
Charlie	Anne Lacey
Helen	Pauline Lockhart
Cal	Robin Laing

Director	Pamela Carter
Assistant Director	Drew Taylor
Sound Designer	Fiona Johnston
Lighting Designer	Nigel Edwards
Technical Manager	Nick Millar

Stage Manager	Gemma Smith
Costume	Helen Murphy

Magic Consultant	Jamie Harrison
Cooking Consultant	Rosie Sykes

**First performed at the Traverse Theatre
Wednesday 17 February 2010**

a Traverse Theatre Commission

THE TRAVERSE

Artistic Director: Dominic Hill

The Traverse has an unrivalled reputation for producing contemporary theatre of the highest quality, invention and energy, and for its dedication to new writing.
(Scotland on Sunday)

The Traverse is Scotland's New Writing Theatre. From its conception in the 1960s, it has embraced a spirit of innovation and risk-taking that launched the careers of many of Scotland's best-known writers including John Byrne, David Greig, David Harrower and Liz Lochhead. It is unique in Scotland in that it fulfils the crucial role of providing the infrastructure, professional support and expertise to ensure the development of a dynamic theatre culture for Scotland.

The Traverse Theatre, the festival's most prestigious home of serious drama. (New York Times)

The Traverse is a pivotal venue in Edinburgh. It receives enormous critical and audience acclaim for its programming, as well as regularly winning awards. In 2009, *Pornography* by Simon Stephens was awarded Best New Play at the Critics' Awards for Theatre in Scotland, making it the second consecutive win for a Traverse production with Alan Wilkins' *Carthage Must Be Destroyed* picking up the award in 2008. From 2001–09, Traverse productions of *Gagarin Way* by Gregory Burke, *Outlying Islands* by David Greig, *Iron* by Rona Munro, *The People Next Door* by Henry Adam, *Shimmer* by Linda McLean, *When the Bulbul Stopped Singing* by Raja Shehadeh, *East Coast Chicken Supper* by Martin J Taylor, *Strawberries in January* by Évelyne de la Chenelière in a version by Rona Munro, *Damascus* by David Greig and *Orphans* by Dennis Kelly have won Fringe First or Herald Angel awards (and occasionally both). Most recently, the Traverse's 2009 Festival programme picked up twenty-one awards including seven Scotsman Fringe Firsts and five Herald Angels.

A Rolls-Royce machine for promoting new Scottish drama across Europe and beyond. (The Scotsman)

The Traverse's success isn't limited to the Edinburgh stage. Since 2001 Traverse productions of *Midsummer*, *Damascus*, *Gagarin Way*, *Outlying Islands*, *Iron*, *The People Next Door*, *When the Bulbul Stopped Singing*, the *Slab Boys Trilogy*, *Mr Placebo* and *Helmet* have toured not only within Scotland and the UK, but in Sweden, Norway, the Balkans, the Middle East, Germany, USA, Iran, Jordan and Canada. In 2009 the Traverse toured its production of *Midsummer (a play with songs)* by David Greig and Gordon McIntyre to Ireland and Canada, with a six-week run at London's Soho Theatre in January 2010.

The Traverse has done Edinburgh proud. (The Observer)

The Traverse's work with young people is of major importance and takes the form of encouraging playwriting through its flagship education project *Class Act*, as well as the Young Writers' Group. *Class Act* is now in its twentieth year and gives school pupils the opportunity to develop their plays with professional playwrights and work with directors and actors to see the finished piece performed on stage at the Traverse. The hugely successful Young Writers' Group is open to new writers aged 18–25, while a newly introduced learning programme, *Scribble*, offers an after-school playwriting and theatre skills workshop for 14–17-year-olds. Both programmes are led by professional playwrights. Following the success of *OutWrite* with young offenders from HMYOI Polmont in 2008, the Traverse will work with participants from HMP Open Estate to improve their literacy and oracy skills through practical drama and playwriting in a project called *OpenWrite*. *OpenWrite* is part of Motherwell College's *Inspiring Change* Project funded by the Scottish Arts Council.

Registered in Scotland (SC076037); registered Charity no. (SC002368)

To find out about ways in which you can support the work of the Traverse, please contact Fiona Sturgeon Shea, Head of Communications, on 0131 228 3223 or fiona.sturgeonshea@traverse.co.uk

www.traverse.co.uk

Ek performance

Ek was founded by Pamela Carter in 2002. Its past projects are *Soul Pilots* (Tramway, 2004), *Habitats* by Philippe Minyana (Tron, 2004), *Plain Speaking* (Tramway, 2005/6) and *Game Theory* by Pamela Carter and Selma Dimitrijević (Traverse and touring, 2007).

Ek is managed by a board of directors, who are Julie Ellen (chair), Andrew Lockyer, Shiona McCubbin, Steve Slater, and Severine Wyper.

Ek is a company limited by guarantee (SC240416) and a registered Scottish charity (SC033931).

For further information please email us at info@by-ek.com

www.by-ek.com

What We Know was made possible with support from the Scottish Arts Council, the McGlashan Charitable Trust, the Federation of Scottish Theatre, Tramway, and the Playwrights' Studio, Scotland.

COMPANY BIOGRAPHIES

Pamela Carter (Writer and Director)

Pamela is a playwright, dramaturg and director. She is the Artistic Director of Ek performance and has devised and directed all of its projects to date. Her plays include *An Argument About Sex* (Untitled/Tramway/Traverse, 2009); *Slope* (Tramway/Untitled, 2006); and *The Last of Us* (Òran Mór, 2008). As a dramaturg, she has worked for Vanishing Point (*Interiors*, Lyric/Traverse, 2009), the National Theatre of Scotland, Malmö Opera House and the Ben Wright Dance Company.

Kate Dickie (*Lucy*)

An award-winning stage and film actress, Kate trained at the Scottish Academy of Music and Drama. Her feature-film debut was *Red Road* for which she received the British Independent Film Award for Best Actress, the Best Actress Award at the Festival du Nouveau Cinema, Montréal, and the BAFTA (Scotland) Best Actress Award. Theatre work includes: *Aalst* (National Theatre of Scotland); *Trojan Women* (Cryptic); *Running Girl* (Boilerhouse); *The Entertainer* (Citizens Theatre). Other film includes: *Outcast, Shelter, Wasted* (Raindog Films); *Somers Town* directed by Shane Meadows; *Summer* directed by Kenneth Glenan; and the forthcoming *Rounding Up Donkeys* directed by Morag MacKinnon. Television includes: *Tinsel Town* (BBC), *Garrow's Law, He Kills Coppers, The Vice*, and the forthcoming *Daughters, The Pillars of the Earth* and *Dive*.

Nigel Edwards (Lighting Designer)

In Britain, Nigel is best known as the lighting designer for Forced Entertainment, having designed eighteen shows since 1990 as well as lighting *That Night Follows Day, Ghent* and *Sight is the Sense* for the company. Other work includes: *Cleansed, 4:48 Psychosis* (Royal Court); *Crave* (Paines Plough); *Roberto Zucco, The Mysteries, Victoria, The Tempest* (RSC); *Dirty Butterfly, Trade, Stoning Mary* (Soho); *Desert Island Dances* (Royal Court Dance); and *Pigg in Hell, Total Masala Slamer, The HCA Project, Solo and Portraits Berlin* (Remote Control): West End shows include: *Sexual Peversity in Chicago, When Harry Met Sally* and *The Postman Always Rings Twice*. Opera includes: *Jenufa* (WNO); and *Hansel and Gretel* (Opera North). Concerts include: Insen and UTP, Ryuichi Sakamoto and Carsten Nicolai, Joss Pook and Diamanda Galas. Nigel also lit Marissa Carnesky's *Ghost Train*.

Paul Thomas Hickey (*Jo*)

For the Traverse: *Passing Places, The Architect, Olga, Greenfields, Slab Boys Trilogy* and European tour of *Gagarin Way*. Other theatre includes: *Monks, All My Sons* (Lyceum); *If Destroyed True, The Talented Mr Ripley, Romeo and Juliet* (Dundee Rep); *The Tempest, San Diego* (Tron); *The*

Entertainer (Citizens Theatre); *Crave, Strawberries in January* (Paines Plough); *Timeless, Mainstream, Killing Time* (Suspect Culture); *Wired* (Òran Mór); *Wasted, Macbeth, A.D., Ecstasy* (Raindog); *Home Hindrance* (Vanishing Point); *Slab Boys Trilogy* (Young Vic); *The Backroom* (Bush); *Shining Souls* (Old Vic). Television and film includes: *The Britoil Fraud, Taggart, Cardiac Arrest, Nightlife, The Bill, Tinsel Town, Hope Springs, Wanting and Getting, California Sunshine, Believe, Wasted* and *The Last Word*.

Fiona Johnston (Sound Designer)

Fiona has a BA in Technical and Production Arts and an MSc in Sound Design. She has a particular interest in composing semi-musical soundscapes through manipulation of found and recorded real-world sounds, and in the effect of sonic art in a live environment. Fiona has designed sound for productions at the Arches, Òran Mór and the Traverse, amongst others. As a Stage Manager, she has a particular interest in working with community and children's theatre, and recently worked for Giant Productions and A Moment's Peace Theatre Company.

Anne Lacey (*Charlie*)

Anne trained in Scotland, France and Italy. For the Traverse: *The Pearlfisher, All this Will Come to Nothing, Dark Earth, The Straw Chair, Bondagers, The Silver Sprig, Shetland Saga, Distracted*. Other theatre includes: *The House of Bernarda Alba* (National Theatre of Scotland); *Men Should Weep* (Oxford Stage); *Victoria* (RSC); *Shining Souls* (Old Vic); *Mary Queen of Scots Got Her Head Chopped Off, The House with the Green Shutters, The Cone Gatherers, Tall Tales, Jack Tamson's Bairns* (Communicado). Anne has also worked with Dundee Rep, the Tron, Òran Mór and the Citizens Theatre, Glasgow. Television includes: *Hamish Macbeth, Monarch of the Glen, Holby City, Tinsel Town, Stacey Stone, Doctor Finlay, Wildflowers, The Real Thing, Knowing the Score* and *Rab C. Nesbitt*. Film includes: *Harry Potter and the Goblet of Fire, This Year's Love, My Life So Far, Strictly Sinatra*, and shorts *Mirror Mirror, Nan, Fishy and the Bedfords*.

Robin Laing (*Cal*)

For the Traverse: *Miles in Nova Scotia, The World is Too Much* and *Ravenhill For Breakfast*. Other theatre includes: *The Elephant Man, Balgay Hill, The Mill Lavvies* (Dundee Rep); *Mary Rose, Living Quarters, All My Sons, The Winter's Tale, Monks, As You Like It* (Lyceum); *Mary Stuart, Elizabeth Gordon Quinn* (National Theatre of Scotland/Lyceum/Citizens Theatre); *Slope* (Untitled Projects/Tramway); *Invention of Love* (Salisbury Playhouse); *Medea* (US tour, Broadway, Paris); *A Midsummer Night's Dream, Loot* (Royal Exchange, Manchester); *Skylight* (Perth Theatre); *Trainspotting* (UK tour/West End). Television includes: *Taggart, Murder*

City (Granada); *Relative Strangers, Heaven on Earth* (Red Rooster/Channel 4); *Born and Bred, Waking the Dead, Into the Blue, The Lakes, Murder Rooms: The Dark Beginnings of Sherlock Holmes* (BBC) and *Band of Brothers* (HBO/Dreamworks). Film includes: *Joyeux Noël, Joy Rider, Borstal Boy, Beautiful Creatures* and *The Slab Boys*. Robin has worked extensively on radio, providing voices for Book of the Week, dramas and readings on Radio Scotland, Radio 3 and Radio 4.

Pauline Lockhart (*Helen*)

Pauline has worked extensively with many of the UK's leading theatre companies including Royal Exchange, Manchester, Hampstead Theatre, West Yorkshire Playhouse, Improbable Theatre, National Theatre of Scotland, Stellar Quines, Suspect Culture, Òran Mór, the Tron, Communicado, Royal Lyceum, Edinburgh, Theatre Babel, Grid Iron, and Ek performance. Television includes: *Holby City, Monarch of the Glen, Casualty* (BBC); *Heartless, The Glass* (ITV). Film includes: *Strictly Sinatra* and *Gladiatress*. Radio includes work for BBC Radio Scotland, Radio 3 and 4. Pauline was awarded the TMA Best Supporting Actress and the Manchester Evening News Award for *An Experiment in an Airpump* (Royal Exchange, Manchester).

Lorn Macdonald (*Teenager*)

Lorn is from Edinburgh and has been a member of Lyceum Youth Theatre (LYT) for nine years. With LYT he has performed at the Traverse, Lyceum and King's Theatres, including National Theatre Connections productions. He was a cast member for the 2008 National Theatre of Scotland/Lyceum/Citizens Theatre co-production of *Six Characters in Search of an Author* and took part in a rehearsed reading of work by Pamela Carter at the Tramway, directed by John Tiffany, in December 2009. Lorn has appeared on film and television and has made several short films, including two which were shown at the 2010 London Short Film Festival in January. He is also a member of young Edinburgh-based company, ineffect.

Nick Millar (Technical Director)

Nick is an artist, technician and production manager working in performance and the visual arts. As a technician and production manager Nick has worked with artists including Nicola Atkinson, Robbie Coleman, Minty Donald, Simon Yuill and companies including Glasgow Sculpture Studios, Glasgow International, the National Theatre of Scotland, Scottish Opera, Untitled Projects, Magnetic North, Quarantine, Traverse Theatre Company, 7:84 Theatre Company and Welfare State International. Although at home in a theatre environment, much of Nick's work is on projects outside of traditional theatre and arts spaces.

Drew Taylor (Assistant Director)
Drew is Artistic Director of proudExposure theatre, a collective of young creatives. Recent projects include: *Sub-Opera* (Subway Festival); *The Family/In His Best Interests* (Arches Scratch); *Natural Selection* (Brunswick Hotel); and a rehearsed reading of *Out Westgate* (PULSE festival). Other directing credits include: *RENT* (Gilmorehill G12); *The Chalky White Substance/The Municipal Abattoir* (Glasgay!/Arches); and *Chaplin* (YMT:UK). Upcoming projects include a new commission for the Glasgay! Festival and a series of new-writing workshops with RSAMD, the Citizens Theatre and Glasgay! Drew will also direct and produce a tour of *Makeover* with Conflux along with two productions at the Edinburgh Festival Fringe. Drew's position as Assistant Director on *What We Know* is suppported by the Federation of Scottish Theatre and the Scottish Arts Council.

SPONSORSHIP AND DEVELOPMENT

We would like to thank the following
corporate funders for their support

New Arts Sponsorship Grants
Supported by the Scottish Government
In conjunction with
A&B
Arts & Business Scotland

Scottish & Newcastle UK

LUMISON

Playwrights'
Studio,
Scotland

To find out how you can benefit from being a Traverse Corporate
Funder, please contact Fiona Sturgeon Shea, Head of
Communications, on 0131 228 3223 or
fiona.sturgeonshea@traverse.co.uk

The Traverse Theatre's work
would not be possible without the support of

Scottish
Arts Council   **BRITISH COUNCIL**   ·EDINBVRGH·
THE CITY OF EDINBURGH COUNCIL

Emerging Playwright on Attachment post supported by
Playwrights' Studio, Scotland as a Partnership Project

Pearson Playwright supported by **Pearson**

The Traverse Theatre receives
financial assistance from:

The Atlantic Philanthropies, The Barcapel Foundation,
The Misses Barrie Charitable Trust, The Binks Trust,
The Craignish Trust, The Cross Trust, The Cruden Foundation,
The Imlay Foundation, James Thom Howat Charitable Trust,
The John Thaw Foundation,
The Lloyds TSB Foundation for Scotland,
The Peggy Ramsay Foundation,
The Ronald Duncan Literary Foundation, Sky Youth Action Fund,
Tay Charitable Trust, The Thistle Trust, The Weatherall Foundation

For their continued generous support of Traverse
productions, the Traverse thanks:

Habitat
Marks and Spencer, Princes Street
Camerabase

For their help on *What We Know*
Ek would like to thank:

Purni Morell, National Theatre Studio, Cal the Trauma Queen,
Alan Wilkins, Mike Bhim, Phil Spencer, Cove Park,
Playwrights' Studio Scotland, Claire Yspol,
Simon Daw, Vanishing Point, Lee Breuer, Maude Mitchell
and SAICA Packaging, Edinburgh

ARE YOU DEVOTED?

Our Devotees are:

Joan Aitken, Stewart Binnie, Katie Bradford, Fiona Bradley, Adrienne Sinclair Chalmers, Lawrence Clark, Adam Fowler, Joscelyn Fox, Caroline Gardner, John Knight OBE, Iain Millar, Gillian Moulton, Helen Pitkethly, Michael Ridings, Bridget Stevens, Walton & Parkinson

The Traverse could not function without the generous support of our patrons. In March 2006, the Traverse Devotees was launched to offer a whole host of exclusive benefits to our loyal supporters

Become a Traverse Devotee for £29 per month or £350 per annum and receive:

- A night at the theatre including six tickets, drinks and a backstage tour
- Your name inscribed on a brick in our wall
- Sponsorship of one of our brand new Traverse 2 seats
- Invitations to Devotees' events
- Your name featured on this page in Traverse Theatre Company scripts and a copy mailed to you
- Free hire of the Traverse Bar Café (subject to availability)

Bricks in our wall and seats in Traverse 2 are also available separately. Inscribed with a message of your choice, these make ideal and unusual gifts.

To join the Devotees or to discuss giving us your support in another way, please contact Fiona Sturgeon Shea, Head of Communications, on 0131 228 3223 or fiona.sturgeonshea@traverse.co.uk

TRAVERSE THEATRE – THE COMPANY

WHAT WE KNOW

Pamela Carter

for kenneth c. carter
and for ed meynell

where did you go?

x

Characters

LUCY
JO, *her partner*
TEENAGER
CHARLIE, *a neighbour*
HELEN, *an emergency-call handler*
CAL, *Lucy's college friend*

A forward slash in the text (/) indicates the point at which the next speaker interrupts.

An ellipsis (…) indicates an unfinished thought or sentence.

This text went to press before the end of rehearsals and so may differ slightly from the play as performed.

evening. a kitchen, lived-in and familiar.

a man and a woman are preparing food.

a meal of semolina gnocchi with a puttanesca sauce followed by blancmange will be cooked and eaten in the real time of the play.

there is music playing: a favourite album.

the man, JO, opens tins of tomatoes, chops onions and garlic. under his direction, LUCY measures quantities of milk, cream and sugar into a saucepan and puts it on the stove to heat. there's also milk in a bowl next to her.

JO. it's unspeakable. sort of.

　　LUCY *stares into the bowl of milk.*

　　or like 'unspeakable' maybe. but nicer.

LUCY. you're sure?

JO. much nicer.

LUCY. squeeze it?

JO. yes, i mean it's not, you know, bad.

LUCY. no?

JO. literally, i mean literally un-speakable. un-sayable.

LUCY (*looking into the saucepan*). it's supposed to look like that?

　　JO *checks his watch, lifts a tea towel covering an unbaked loaf of bread on a tray.*

JO. look like what?

LUCY. cum.

JO. give me a second.

LUCY. no, cum.

> JO *puts the bread into the oven.*

JO. what?

LUCY. is it supposed to look like cum?

JO. i don't know. yes. well, why not?

LUCY. really?

JO. looks fine to me.

> *he arranges ingredients around him: olives, capers, chilli, herbs, sugar, vinegar.*
>
> it was… it was… in, in, in… oh. (*he indicates his mouth*) i can feel it here, you know. f… f… f… there's fuff in it.
>
> it used to be here. you know, it's a bit like this, what's happening now.

LUCY. what is happening?

JO. not finding the words for something.

LUCY. not that.

JO. an idea or a feeling…

LUCY. i mean this.

JO. if you can't put it into words –

LUCY. what's this about?

JO. it escapes.

LUCY. right.

> *she lifts something out of the bowl of milk with her hand.*
>
> christ.

JO. squeeze.

LUCY. ewww. in there?

JO. yep.

she drops the gelatine into the saucepan.

LUCY. what i meant is have i missed something? is it a special occasion or something?

JO. every day with you is special.

she stirs the mixture.

LUCY. this can't be right.

JO. it can.

LUCY. show me the recipe.

JO. there isn't one.

LUCY. so how do you know?

JO. what?

LUCY. it'll work.

JO. i just do.

LUCY. look.

JO. trust me.

LUCY. no idea, have you?

JO. yes.

LUCY. not a fucking clue.

JO. i can feel it. i can feel it in my –

LUCY. bollocks.

JO. well, perhaps.

LUCY. smug twat.

JO. want some reassurance?

he goes to take hold of her.

LUCY (*laughing*). fuck off.

JO. you worry too much.

he looks at what she's making.

LUCY. and?

JO. i see what you mean.

LUCY *shows him her hand.*

LUCY. even dries like spunk.

he takes her hand to lick it.

JO. yum.

LUCY. get off.

JO. it's okay.

LUCY. yeah?

JO. it'll be fine.

LUCY. you always say that.

JO. i like fine.

LUCY. because it's not. not always.

JO. no, sometimes it's better. much better.

you're doing a grand job. it's spot on. it'll be delicious, you'll see.

he puts a frying pan on the stove and some oil in to heat.

pass me that.

LUCY. what?

JO. the thingy.

LUCY. what thingy?

JO. the thingy.

he gestures. she holds up a large spoon.

not scoopy.

LUCY. scrapy?

JO. that's the fellow.

she throws a spatula to him.

ta.

he slides the onions and garlic into the pan to cook.

LUCY. how do i know when it's ready?

JO. know what?

LUCY. when it's ready.

JO. the same way you know anything's ready.

LUCY. you'll tell me.

he hums/sings to himself. she watches him.

why are you so chirpy?

JO. it's my job, isn't it?

LUCY. and pudding.

JO. i do the light; you do the shade.

LUCY. but 'nothing special'.

JO. light, shade. it's texture.

LUCY. it's lumpy.

JO. i don't know. i suppose, i thought we might extend our repertoire this weekend.

a little domestic adventure. the two of us. nothing wrong with that, is there?

LUCY. we'll see, won't we?

JO. making lovely food together. that's good, isn't it?

she spills a little of the blancmange mixture.

LUCY. tits.

JO. here.

he throws her a cloth.

f... f... f... aghh. f.

he pats himself as if looking for his wallet.

this keeps happening. you know the feeling of something and you go to get it but it's not there. at least, it's not where i thought it'd be. it happens to you too.

LUCY. losing things?

JO. words.

she wipes herself.

LUCY. cock.

JO. you don't swear any less.

LUCY. got a problem with that?

JO. not at all. i love your dirty mouth.

LUCY. good.

JO. i wouldn't change it for the world.

LUCY. good.

JO. you might though. if things were different.

LUCY. where?

JO. you know... if there were impressionable minds around.

LUCY. meaning?

JO. you know... children.

LUCY. here?

JO. yes.

LUCY. well, there aren't.

JO. no, but if there were.

LUCY. but there aren't.

JO. they're so absorbent.

LUCY. where have the children come from?

JO. nowhere. i'm just speculating, you know... what with you being so uncouth.

she flicks him the finger.

but economical with it.

LUCY. you bullshit enough for the both of us.

JO. a winning combination of base and lofty.

she throws the cloth back to him.

so have we? lost words?

LUCY. us?

JO. yes. do you think we say less?

LUCY. maybe there's less to talk about.

JO. we've run out of things to talk about?

LUCY. i didn't mean it like that.

JO. there's no need to talk as much?

LUCY. maybe.

JO. we don't need so many words.

she shrugs.

we're not the same as we were, say, six years ago. are we? we didn't know each other six years ago.

LUCY. no.

JO. i'm not the same... i sleep better. i eat better. i eat more. i laugh more. i know more. i care more. i've gained. i'm a better, happier person. there's nothing lost there.

he hums/sings to himself, adds a splash of sherry vinegar to the onions and cooks it off.

where do they go? it's a good question, don't you think?

words. where've they gone?

LUCY. it's just forgetting. it's what happens.

JO. do you think we've fused over time?

LUCY. you've said this before.

JO. rubbing together.

LUCY. i'm not you.

JO. i know. and that's good.

he empties the tins of tomatoes into his pan and stirs.

has our world shrunk then? what do you think? do we say less because actually there is less?

LUCY. i don't think less. inside. i don't feel less.

JO. no, neither do i.

so what are you thinking about?

LUCY. nothing.

JO. well then.

LUCY. nothing much.

JO. tell me.

LUCY. do i have to?

JO. please.

LUCY holds a ladle up.

LUCY. you want to know what i'm thinking right now?

JO. no. before.

LUCY. before when?

JO. before then. you were holding the spoon like this.

he demonstrates.

LUCY. do I really look like that?

JO. don't change the subject.

she finds the position JO *has indicated she was 'thinking' in.*

LUCY. really, nothing interesting.

JO. not true.

LUCY. bollocks.

JO. try me.

LUCY. no.

JO. you were looking over there.

LUCY *moves her head.*

no, before that. chin down – that's it. and you moved your shoulder. back. that's it.

LUCY *thinks.*

LUCY. heat.

JO. temperature.

LUCY. i was thinking if it was too high. or too low.

JO. getting it right?

LUCY. yes. and something about the car.

JO. you're good to go. it's ready.

LUCY *lifts the saucepan.*

LUCY. okay in here?

LUCY *pours the contents of the pan into the glass bowl.*

JO. so? what about me?

LUCY. what about you?

JO. don't you want to know?

LUCY. what?

JO. you're such a tease.

LUCY. please tell me. what are you thinking about?

JO. only if you're sure?

LUCY. would i ask if i wasn't?

JO. honest?

LUCY. always.

JO. you really want to know?

LUCY. desperately. like i'd keel over and fucking die if you didn't tell me what was frittering about in that pretty little head of yours.

JO. alright then. when?

LUCY. just then. you were… this.

she holds up her right hand and looks at it. JO *stares at his for a moment and thinks.*

JO. people. i think.

LUCY. what people?

JO. it's complicated.

LUCY. goes without saying.

JO. it starts when you say 'heat'. because then i look at my hand. the burn.

LUCY. it's okay?

JO. yes, yes. it's my skin. i'm looking at my skin, its… outsideness. and then i think about what's inside. meat, bones, fat.

chemicals and electricity. the fizz and the tick. you know, all of this you can measure, one way or another.

and then. then i think about what makes me more than a skin bag of bones and blood. you know, lessons i've learned, fights i've had, why ketchup and not brown sauce, everything i've forgotten, what i want to happen next, the people i know…

LUCY. right.

JO. so, people.

LUCY. got you.

JO. no but that's not it. it doesn't finish there. no, because where do you stop? (*pinching the skin on his hand*) not here.

> LUCY *stirs the liquid in the glass bowl. then she begins to clear up around her.*

> this isn't the end of it at all. i go beyond, to you, to what's out there. i'm more than this...

LUCY. of course you are.

JO. we are. we're more dispersed and more massive than this. there's so much. i have so much.

> and it's so delicate, detailed. and then i thought it must be the same for them.

LUCY. 'them'?

JO. other people. with hands. well, skin at least. it's the same for them. don't you think?

LUCY. you'd think so. the parking vouchers.

JO. all those people. billions of them. all those people out there living lives in as much detail as we do.

> it's immense. and exciting.

LUCY. did you pick up the parking vouchers?

JO. no.

LUCY. oh, for / fuck's sake.

JO. go on, you have to think that's exciting?

LUCY. you said / you would...

JO. don't change the subject.

LUCY. me?

JO. you have to think that's exciting.

LUCY. you don't get out of it like that.

JO. go on. it's exciting.

LUCY. is it?

JO. the scale. the abundance.

LUCY. maybe.

JO. well, what then? if it isn't exciting.

LUCY. i think… i think… it's too big. too much.

JO. too much?

LUCY. over…

JO. overwhelming.

LUCY. yes.

JO. numbers?

LUCY. no.

JO. what then?

LUCY. the responsibility.

JO. that abundance makes you feel responsible?

LUCY. no.

JO. so?

LUCY. thinking about it. knowing it's there. once you know it's there…

JO. the responsibility is overwhelming.

LUCY. something like that.

JO. ah.

    JO *looks at* LUCY *for a few moments*.

LUCY. what?

JO. nothing.

he tastes the sauce and seasons it with salt and pepper.

LUCY. what?

JO. nothing.

he tastes the sauce again.

lovely.

LUCY. what? tell me.

JO. no. i know when to keep quiet.

LUCY. like fuck you do.

he starts to tidy, putting used crockery in the sink, wiping surfaces.

say it.

JO. no.

LUCY. say it.

JO. no.

LUCY. you will.

JO. won't.

LUCY. any fucking money.

JO. nothing to say.

LUCY. ha.

JO. in. f... f... f... ferble.

he bangs his head with his hand.

you know what your problem is, / don't you?

LUCY. see. ha. see. pompous prick.

JO. remind me why i love you.

LUCY. screw you.

JO. okay.

he continues tidying.

LUCY. so, what then?

JO. what 'what then'?

LUCY. bastard.

JO. what?

LUCY. you know.

JO. know what?

LUCY. my problem? what's my fucking problem then?

JO. ah yes.

LUCY. what? tell me.

JO. nah.

LUCY. tell me.

JO. say please.

LUCY. fucker.

JO. not unless you say please.

LUCY. fuck-face.

JO. right then.

LUCY. we'll see.

they both busy themselves.

(whispered) f… f… f… ineff –

JO. you see your problem / is…

LUCY. ah ha. ha. you see. couldn't resist, could you? i fucking /
    know you.

JO. your problem / is…

LUCY. like a book.

JO. your problem –

LUCY. no, your problem... your problem is... because this is
no revelation, you know, (*waving her hands in the air*) that
other people have hands too.

JO. i know.

LUCY. fuck, that's it. your problem is that you can't believe
that anyone else might be as fascinating to themselves, or to
anyone else for that matter, as you are to you. yeah.

JO. so you're saying i'm a wanker?

LUCY. i didn't say that.

JO. you're saying i'm self-obsessed?

LUCY. not necessarily.

JO. that i only think about myself.

LUCY. no.

JO. because i don't.

LUCY. i know that.

JO. i think about everything else as well as myself.

LUCY. parking vouchers.

JO. maybe not / that...

LUCY. and i didn't mean it like that.

JO. well, how then?

LUCY. i meant how do you find yourself / so...

JO. it's not just me.

LUCY. so persistently surprising.

JO. i have a sense of wonder.

LUCY. yes.

JO. and that's endearing.

LUCY. it is?

JO. you've always said it was endearing.

LUCY. yes, it is. it's like living with an amnesiac puppy.

JO. you can surprise yourself, you know.

LUCY. you think?

JO. you have no idea what you do.

LUCY. i don't do anything.

JO. much more than you realise.

LUCY. i just get on with stuff.

JO. that's your problem.

LUCY. what?

JO. you look at the world and you think you're invisible to it. you think you can look at it but that it doesn't look back at you. i'll pick them up first thing monday. promise.

LUCY. why should it?

JO. you've got no idea what you do. and that's endearing.

he puts away jars, bottles.

LUCY. ineffable.

JO. what was that?

LUCY. the word you were looking for. ineffable.

JO *hits his hand against his head.*

JO. ineffable. of course. of course, it is. ineffable. thank you, darling.

LUCY. it had to be here somewhere.

JO. sweetheart. look at this. we have all of this… these… this…

ingredients, tools, this heat, these hands. and they're all perfect. sort of. they all work. we can put them together and make them work. we can do that. look at what we have, what the possibilities are. laksa. ceviche. sachertorte. koulibiac. beautiful things to say and make and eat.

LUCY. we're lucky.

JO. everything is good.

LUCY. but?

JO. no buts.

LUCY. good.

JO. how much do you love me?

LUCY. you know.

JO. i know you love me. at least i think i do.

LUCY. there you go then.

JO. but you could tell me. you could say it. go on. just for fun.

LUCY. stop it. i'm not like you.

JO. surprise yourself. how much do you love me? try.

LUCY. no.

JO. i'll help you. let's measure it. a spoonful? tablespoon? a ladleful?

LUCY. you're such a twat.

JO. this much? (*he holds up a bag of sugar*) half a pound, say?

or do you prefer metric?

LUCY. i don't know.

JO. so. less precise and harder to judge. a handful maybe? a dash? just a pinch?

LUCY *is laughing*.

will feed six? no? two for a light lunch? go on. tell me. how much?

LUCY. jesus. this much.

she indicates a couple of inches with her fingers.

about six inches, you'd say.

JO. you're a cruel woman.

he stirs his sauce.

LUCY. you just fancy blancmange all of a sudden?

JO. honest. everything's fa fa fa fine. perfect. we… we… we…

we have so much. all this space. the two of us. all of this. imagine.

LUCY. imagine what?

JO. ineffable.

LUCY. what is?

he bangs the heel of his hand against his forehead.

JO. imagine. someone new in this world. to our world. we'd have to teach them the words for it.

LUCY. what are you trying to say?

JO. here we are rattling round this space, with all this to share. and we can do whatever we want, make whatever we want. make this. call it dumplings, call it gnocchi. all good stuff, right?

LUCY. okay.

she puts the blancmange in the fridge to set.

JO. we could leave out all the bad stuff.

LUCY. what… shit.

LUCY *knocks something to the floor.*

i'm so fucking clumsy. bollocks. what was that?

she starts to clear the mess up.

what was that again? jo?

she stands and turns to face JO.

i don't get it. jo? what are you doing?

JO *has disappeared, suddenly and completely, as if by magic.*

what's going on? where are you?

the kitchen is exactly the same as it was a few seconds ago: however, nothing is as it was previously. everything has changed. LUCY *recognises absolutely nothing around her.*

 jo. stop fucking about. where are you?

a teenage boy appears from nowhere.

TEENAGER. what's up?

LUCY. who…?

TEENAGER. door was open…

the TEENAGER *wanders about looking at the food.*

what you cooking?

LUCY. where…?

the TEENAGER *pulls a rolled-up newspaper from his sleeve and drops it on the table.*

TEENAGER. all part of the service.

LUCY. jo?

TEENAGER. i'm lee. totally lee, man.

LUCY. lee.

TEENAGER. or hank.

LUCY. hm?

TEENAGER. hank in extremis.

LUCY. i…

TEENAGER. marvin. starving. get it? yeah. so i don't suppose you got anything i can eat, like?

LUCY *is also looking around her, touching unfamiliar objects, bumping into things.*

LUCY. fuck.

TEENAGER. i was only asking.

LUCY. fucking hell.

TEENAGER. woah. no need for that, man. i was only asking. that's not right. you're a grown-up. i'm a minor. grown-ups not supposed to talk to a minor like that, man. not setting the right tone. not leading by example.

LUCY. jesus fucking christ.

TEENAGER. woah. that ain't nice. profaning, man. not nice. not nice at all.

he tuts to himself as he inspects the sauce cooking on the stove. LUCY *looks about her, bewildered.*

LUCY. what the hell is going on here? what is this?

TEENAGER (*shrugging*). it's your kitchen.

LUCY. this isn't it. this isn't how it's supposed to be.

TEENAGER. smells funny in here, eh? don't you think it smells funny in here?

LUCY. and you.

TEENAGER. nah, not me, man. no way.

LUCY. no.

TEENAGER. i can smell something. not like edible smells, like. (*he indicates the food*) not that, like.

LUCY. you're not jo.

TEENAGER. burning. that's it.

LUCY. he's not here.

TEENAGER. yeah, i can smell something burning, man.

LUCY. what's happening?

TEENAGER. i think there's something burning.

LUCY. what?

TEENAGER. hot... fire... you know... burning.

LUCY. oh fuck. christ no. oh, fucking hell. oh fuck. fuck. fuck. no.

she runs backwards and forwards for a few moments until she heads to the oven and retrieves the burning bread.

TEENAGER (*imitating the sound of a fire engine*). nee-naw-nee-naw...

LUCY. be okay. be okay. please be okay. oh fuck. shit.

TEENAGER. nee-naw, nee-naw. having a barbecue...

LUCY. you. shit. oh shit. i can't. this can't. fucking hell. fuck. no. fuck.

TEENAGER. calm down, man.

LUCY. no. don't do this to me.

TEENAGER. just a bit of burning. be cool.

LUCY dumps the burnt bread out onto a surface.

LUCY. this isn't supposed to fucking happen.

TEENAGER. chill. (*he laughs*) that's funny. get it?

LUCY. not like this.

TEENAGER. coool. uncooool.

LUCY. i don't understand.

TEENAGER. hot and cold, like. burning. cool. they's opposite. like a joke. funny. ha ha.

LUCY. this is a joke?

TEENAGER. gotta have a sense of humour, man.

she stares at him for a few seconds.

LUCY. what have you done?

TEENAGER. eh?

LUCY. what have you done?

TEENAGER. nothing. i was just having a laugh, just trying to lighten the tone.

LUCY. we were here.

TEENAGER. nothing wrong with lightening the tone.

LUCY. i went… (*she turns to the fridge*) and then I dropped… (*she indicates the place she dropped the plate onto the floor*) and then…

TEENAGER. nothing wrong with that.

LUCY. and then you.

TEENAGER. the door was open.

LUCY. what have you done?

TEENAGER. nothing.

LUCY. you must have done something.

TEENAGER. that's not fair, man. i didn't touch nothing. it's not my fault your bread's burnt.

LUCY. everything was fine.

TEENAGER. oh, man. just cos i'm the youth. you people think you got the right to blame us / for everything.

LUCY. everything was just fine. / he said so.

TEENAGER. this is a police state, man. i didn't / touch nothing.

LUCY. he was right here in / front of me.

TEENAGER. it's not fair. i am / innocent.

LUCY. we were just / talking.

TEENAGER. miscarriage of / justice.

LUCY. jo was / talking.

TEENAGER. i done nothing / wrong.

LUCY. and we were cooking.

TEENAGER. not me.

LUCY. and then you.

TEENAGER. nah, it's you. you got it wrong. blaming me for things i ain't done. making me out to be some kind of criminal. i was just trying to help. being nice. telling you about the burning.

LUCY. i'm right here.

TEENAGER. nothing wrong with me.

LUCY. jo's there.

TEENAGER. it's you. with your language, and your weird-nesses and your 'jo this' and your 'jo that'.

LUCY. so stop pissing about and tell me where he fucking is then.

TEENAGER. how do i know? i don't know anyone called jo. who's jo?

LUCY. what?

TEENAGER. who's jo when he's at home?

LUCY. jo?

TEENAGER. what difference it gonna make anyway?

LUCY. he's...

TEENAGER. what?

LUCY. not here.

   the TEENAGER *looks around him.*

TEENAGER. evidently.

they stare at each other.

LUCY. are you sure you don't know / where he is?

TEENAGER. aw, man. i / keep saying…

LUCY. you see, he was / just here and…

TEENAGER. you think i'm a liar and i'm not a liar. i am telling the truth. i always tell the truth. not fair calling me / a liar.

LUCY. no, i didn't say / that…

TEENAGER. it's not fair. i am a honest person.

LUCY. okay.

TEENAGER. i am a truthful person.

LUCY. yes, alright.

TEENAGER. i'm hurt, man.

LUCY. look, i'm sorry. i didn't mean to… i didn't mean… i mean… it's probably nothing, really, it's just that something strange is happening. i think.

TEENAGER. you don't say.

LUCY. jo… joseph edward rain. he's thirty-five. april 6th 1974. not married but we're together, he lives here with me, he's my partner.

he was right here where he usually is. but now, i don't know. because now he's…

TEENAGER. like, gone.

LUCY. he's not here. he's not anywhere.

TEENAGER. like, 'see ya later'.

LUCY. he didn't say anything. no warning.

TEENAGER. like magic.

LUCY. with me. and then not.

TEENAGER. pfiff.

LUCY. how is that?

TEENAGER. spooky.

LUCY. he wouldn't just leave me.

the TEENAGER *is looking for something to eat.*

maybe i missed something. maybe he did say something and I misunderstood.

TEENAGER. mebbe.

he picks up a jar of capers.

LUCY. maybe i wasn't listening properly. oh god.

he takes the lid off and sniffs the contents of the jar.

TEENAGER. aw, man.

he picks up an olive.

LUCY. think. think. what did he say? he was standing there. you.

TEENAGER (*throwing the olive away*). didn't touch anything.

LUCY. come here.

she takes his elbow, leads him to the spot where JO *had stood and steps back to look at him.*

there. standing there. holding, holding a... yes, because there's this...

she indicates the 'v' between her thumb and forefinger of her right hand. she gives the TEENAGER *a spoon.*

like this. yes. okay. words. names. i turned and i bent here and i took the... said 'why?' and he said, he said something. and me, up and turned. and then... nothing.

TEENAGER. awesome.

LUCY. people don't just disappear.

TEENAGER. no?

LUCY. they don't just vanish. into thin air.

TEENAGER. pfiff.

LUCY. he had a thing. today. about words.

the TEENAGER *goes to move.*

no.

TEENAGER. not doing anything.

LUCY. yes, that's it. (*she repositions him*) and he's naming
food. saying the names of different dishes.

TEENAGER. nice.

LUCY. delicious names.

TEENAGER. pizza. how's that?

LUCY. he says. says. something about having room, making
room for something else, someone else. having words.

TEENAGER. pie.

LUCY. i turned and i bent here, and i took the, said... i said...

TEENAGER. meat pie.

LUCY. 'i don't get it.'

TEENAGER. pie and chips.

LUCY. and then he's gone.

TEENAGER. chips.

LUCY. he didn't say he was going.

TEENAGER. just chips.

LUCY. he would've said.

TEENAGER. makes you hungry this, eh?

LUCY. because he thinks about me. whatever he does, it
includes me. that's how it works.

TEENAGER. cool. (*looking at the sauce*) is that tomato?

LUCY. he wouldn't have just left me.

TEENAGER. loads of food here.

LUCY. look at all this.

TEENAGER. looks well dodgy.

LUCY. what am i supposed to do?

TEENAGER. eat it? bit much for just you, mind.

LUCY. what do you mean?

TEENAGER. on your jack jones.

LUCY. what are you saying?

TEENAGER. otherwise you'd be a bit number 8.

LUCY. what do you mean?

TEENAGER. a fat lady.

LUCY. don't you fucking say that.

TEENAGER. say what? i didn't / say you...

LUCY. do you think i'm stupid?

TEENAGER. aw, no. i didn't / say you're...

LUCY. do you think i'm fucking stupid?

TEENAGER. no.

LUCY. of course i can't eat it on my fucking own. i've got no
intention of eating it on my fucking own because i'm not on
my fucking own.

what the fuck is everyone's problem? christ, you dare... how
dare you look at me like i'm stupid... like i'm out of my
fucking mind or something.

how in god's fucking name could i eat this on my fucking
own? of course it's not just for me, you stupid thoughtless
fucking hell fuck... jesus. shit. sorry. shit.

they look at each other for a few moments.

TEENAGER. i don't think you should have really said that to me.

LUCY. no.

TEENAGER. in fact, i think you might have overstepped the mark a bit there.

LUCY. yes.

TEENAGER. crossed the rubicon.

LUCY. yes.

TEENAGER. cos it's not my fault.

LUCY. no.

TEENAGER. i got a really fast metabolism.

LUCY. i'm sorry.

TEENAGER. super-fast. like lightning. it's because i'm young. still growing.

LUCY. you're what?

TEENAGER. maturing. it's annoying, like, cos i don't want to eat all the time but i got no choice. it's my metabolic rate, see.

i'm like a machine, digesting all the time. just burning fuel. i don't want to eat all the time but i have to.

LUCY. you're hungry.

TEENAGER. it's inconvenient. but i gotta put fuel in the engine. i gotta eat or i'm gonna break down, you know. stop working.

LUCY. you want me to give you some food.

TEENAGER. malfunction. got no choice. just the way i am. scooting about, shooting the breeze, generating all this energy.

LUCY. okay.

TEENAGER. all this electricity. standing still, even, minding my own business, i'm still breathing, still growing. can't help it.

LUCY. okay.

TEENAGER. i gotta eat when i need to cos / otherwise...

LUCY. i said, okay. okay. just not this.

TEENAGER....i'll waste away, man.

LUCY. this is not for you.

she takes a dish out of the fridge.

TEENAGER. fade away. like expire. go to meet my maker. shuffle off this moral... this mortal...

she puts the dish down in front of him.

...thingy. what's that?

LUCY. it's koulibiac.

TEENAGER. who?

LUCY. koulibiac. pie.

TEENAGER. what kind of pie?

LUCY. fish pie.

TEENAGER. ugh. not eating fish, man. fish is disgusting. all slimy and their goggly eyes. no way. ugh.

LUCY. there's rice in it as well.

TEENAGER. aw, man. what kind of pie has rice in it? that's not a pie; that's a tragedy.

LUCY. f. well, what then?

TEENAGER. i dunno. got anything sweet, like? i got a sweet tooth, me. i like a bit of cake. or a bit of pie with apple in it. now that's a pie, apple pie. if you've got any apple pie...

she takes the koulibiac to the fridge and pulls out a bowl.

i got a savoury tooth too, mind. eat anything, me. a machine.

LUCY. not sure this is ready yet.

she puts the bowl down in front of him. he looks at it.

TEENAGER. aw, man. that's rank.

LUCY. what's wrong?

TEENAGER. that's minging.

LUCY. what's wrong with it?

TEENAGER. look at it. look. it looks like… you know…

LUCY. what?

TEENAGER. you know…

LUCY. no…

TEENAGER. jizz.

LUCY. what? oh. it's supposed to look like that.

TEENAGER. that's so wrong. that's sick, man.

she looks at it.

LUCY. yeah, okay.

she takes it back to the fridge.

TEENAGER. aw, man.

LUCY. tell me then. what do you want?

TEENAGER. got any cheese?

LUCY. what kind of cheese?

TEENAGER. cheesy cheese. no funny stuff.

she takes some cheese from the fridge and puts it down in front of him.

cool.

got any bread?

she puts the burnt loaf in front of him and gives him a bread knife.

ta.

he sets about the bread, cutting off the burnt bits, singing dizzee rascal's 'dance wiv me' as he goes. he fashions a sandwich of sorts.

got any ketchup?

LUCY *gets it for him.*

ta.

he puts ketchup on his sandwich and then eats it.

got any juice?

LUCY. what?

TEENAGER. juice?

LUCY *goes to the fridge and gets out some juice. she pours a glass and gives it to him.*

cheers.

she pours herself some and sits.

LUCY. maybe he had some sort of premonition.

TEENAGER. a what?

LUCY. premonition.

TEENAGER. what's one of them?

LUCY. it's a sort of feeling you get. an anxious feeling. when something bad is about to happen, and you can feel it coming.

TEENAGER. like when you don't eat. i get those all the time. the premonitions. nice.

LUCY. was he trying to tell me? that things would change?

TEENAGER. mebbe.

LUCY. he was excited about how much we have. yes. and he had a thing about words. remembering them. sharing them. making space for someone else…

do i know you?

TEENAGER. sure.

he has finished his sandwich.

feeling much better now. brand new. off the hook. what with the cheese and that. cool.

it was close, mind. was beginning to feel a bit wooo, a bit pete tong, like. but i'm good to go now. feeling great. cheers. lifesaver and all that.

LUCY *is stirring the tomato sauce.*

LUCY. was there something else i should have done?

TEENAGER. nah, i'm good.

LUCY. it's not right. i know it's not supposed to be like this but i can't make it work any differently. i think if i think harder, close my eyes and think harder, and then… (*she closes her eyes and opens them*)…but nothing. see. it's still wrong.

TEENAGER. it's just food.

LUCY. what the f… am i supposed to do with this? i don't know what to do.

TEENAGER. don't stress, man.

LUCY. and i don't know why. i don't know why. there are no good answers.

i shouldn't be doing this on my own.

TEENAGER. i'm here.

LUCY. why?

TEENAGER. well, the way i see it, if you want my opinion that is, you know, if you're looking for my advice, well, what i'd say to you is, personally speaking like, what i'd say…

LUCY. ...is what?

TEENAGER. if you don't like the business...

LUCY. yes...

TEENAGER. then get out of the business... blow it out.

LUCY. you'd blow it out?

TEENAGER. you don't like it, don't do it. simple.

LUCY. stop?

TEENAGER. if that's the way you want to put it. this tomato malarky, you don't have to do it, do you? i've had my sandwich and... (*indicating the sauce*) i don't mean no disrepect or anything but i don't really fancy the look of that.

so if you're not into it then just def it. jack it in.

LUCY. and do what?

TEENAGER. whatever you want. nothing.

LUCY *looks around her.*

LUCY. i can do that?

TEENAGER. you're a grown-up. you are master of your own destiny. there's no one telling you to eat your peas. no one telling you to wash behind your ears.

LUCY. no.

TEENAGER. you can do whatever you want, dude.

LUCY. i can.

TEENAGER. you don't like the ride, get off the bus.

LUCY. it's that simple.

TEENAGER. yeah.

she considers this for a while.

LUCY. and what would i do?

TEENAGER. dunno. go find your fella?

LUCY. find jo?

TEENAGER. right.

LUCY. i could. i could do that, couldn't i? leave all this and go look for jo. what's there to stop me?

TEENAGER. nothing.

LUCY. it's that easy.

TEENAGER. lemon squeezy.

LUCY. i'm very tired.

TEENAGER. take a break, put your feet up, turn the light out, close your eyes.

LUCY. i hate this.

TEENAGER. check out of here. walk out that door. don't turn around now.

LUCY *thinks, then laughs to herself. the* TEENAGER *starts to laugh with her.*

LUCY. okay.

TEENAGER. okay.

LUCY. i get it.

TEENAGER. excellent.

LUCY. i see what you're up to.

TEENAGER. cool.

LUCY. very good.

TEENAGER. sweet.

LUCY. it's a test.

TEENAGER. yeah?

LUCY. you're testing me.

TEENAGER. right.

LUCY. testing my resolve.

TEENAGER. i'm here to help.

LUCY. because what would happen if jo came back and i
    wasn't here?

the TEENAGER *shrugs.*

there'd be no one here. nothing ready for him. no food.
nothing. and so why would he come back? why would he if
there's nothing for him to come back to?

so i can't leave. because he is coming back.

TEENAGER. right.

LUCY. i'm staying here.

TEENAGER. you gotta do what you gotta do. and i respect
    that. i will support you in your decision.

LUCY. thank you... what did you say your name was again?

TEENAGER. you ever seen a dead body?

LUCY. no.

TEENAGER. i saw a dead body once.

he points to a dining table, the leaves folded down.

this over here?

LUCY. er, yes.

TEENAGER. no kidding.

he waits at one end of the table for LUCY *to take hold of the
other.*

it was years ago back when i was young, right? and i'm
playing out in these fields. and there's this stream with a
pond, like, and a big pipe across it you can stand on. really
big. massive.

they lift the table between them and stand facing each other.

so i'm sat up on this pipe and checking out the view. you know, sun's shining, sky's blue. and i'm looking in the pond, right?

this way.

they carry the table to the spot the TEENAGER *wants it placed.*

cos people chuck random stuff in there or there are animals or cars, you know, and it's interesting. but sometimes no and it's just rubbish and so i'm having a butcher's and i see this dummy, you know? like a dummy from a shop. and i think 'oh look, someone's thrown a dummy in here.'

but then, there's this moment, right? really radical. you can put the table down now.

they put it down.

ta. you know, when you look at something and it's one thing and then you're still looking at it and it's not that thing any more; it's the same but then it's totally different? same – different. same – different. you with me?

LUCY. i think so.

the TEENAGER *sets four chairs around the table.*

TEENAGER. so one minute i'm looking at a dummy like from a shop, you know. and the next minute, it's a woman.

LUCY. a woman?

TEENAGER. yeah. a real woman. a real dead woman. your sauce…

LUCY. oh.

she checks on the sauce.

TEENAGER. and it's really freaky, man, because I know that she's like dead just like in a film. and it's not a film because it's real but it is like a film because everything's a bit slow-motion-y and a bit woooo.

it's like i'm a camera and i'm zooming in and out, you know, on this dead woman. like she's getting bigger and then smaller. close up and then far away, you know. ooooooop and then waaaaay. do you know what i'm saying?

LUCY. yes, i think so.

TEENAGER. it's wild cos like i can do it now. like the whole thing's like my own personal film in my own head and i can like freeze it and go 'oooooop' and then 'waaaaay'. in my own head. well cool.

well, not for her. cos she was dead. it wasn't cool for her or anything, obviously. because that would be sick, like. not right.

LUCY. that's terrible.

TEENAGER. yeah. extreme stuff. awesome.

LUCY. weren't you frightened?

TEENAGER. of what?

LUCY. i don't know.

TEENAGER. all in a day's work.

LUCY. you see it on the news or in the paper, don't you? someone out for a walk, someone on their way home finds or stumbles… they stumble across a body. i go for walks, i come home all the time but i've never found a body. does that make me lucky or unlucky? because it always happens to other people, doesn't it? and it sort of makes them special, by association. someone else's misfortune.

who was she?

TEENAGER. the dead woman?

LUCY. yes. what happened to her?

TEENAGER. she slipped

LUCY. she fell in?

TEENAGER. yeah.

LUCY. that's very sad. how sad for her.

TEENAGER. too true.

LUCY. why did you tell me that?

TEENAGER. just a bit of banter. just making conversation. you gave me cheese so i thought maybe i should like say something. thought you might want to hear a story. it's good to talk, innit? a bit of food, a bit of chat. it's nice. civilised.

LUCY. lee, where did you come from?

TEENAGER. i dunno. the fairies left me?

the oven 'bings'.

hey. grub's up.

LUCY. already?

TEENAGER. right here, right now…

LUCY. oh, fuck –

TEENAGER. hey.

LUCY. sorry. i'm sorry.

she pulls the tray of gnocchi from the oven. the TEENAGER *looks at it.*

TEENAGER. aw, man.

LUCY. i'd better get on. excuse me.

she sets about finishing the preparation of the meal.

TEENAGER. gotta boost anyway.

LUCY. what was that?

TEENAGER. gotta bust a groove. make a move.

LUCY. you're leaving?

TEENAGER. yeah.

LUCY. oh. you don't have to go. please stay; if you want to, that is.

TEENAGER. appreciate the offer. ta. but i got stuff to do, places to stink up, you know.

LUCY. sure.

TEENAGER. cool meeting you and all that.

LUCY. thank you. yes, you too.

TEENAGER. cheers for the cheese.

LUCY. no problem. thanks for… um…

TEENAGER. the banter? my pleasure.

LUCY. will you be coming back?

TEENAGER. back here?

LUCY. dropping by again?

TEENAGER. i dunno.

LUCY. if you get hungry, you know…

TEENAGER. yeah. feed the machine.

LUCY. you're welcome.

TEENAGER. cheers, like.

LUCY. so… this is it.

TEENAGER. see you later, alligator.

he disappears, leaving LUCY *alone.*

LUCY. bye.

CHARLIE, *a woman in her late fifties, enters the kitchen.*

CHARLIE. here i am.

LUCY. oh.

CHARLIE. it is eight.

LUCY. is it?

CHARLIE. you did say eight. but if you've changed your mind... oh.

> HELEN, *a woman in her thirties, enters the kitchen. she has a plastic bag with a bottle of wine in it.*

HELEN. hello.

LUCY. jesus.

HELEN. oh. is this a bad time?

CHARLIE (*to* HELEN). it's eight. (*to* LUCY) so if it's an inconvenience...

LUCY. no, no. please... (*to* HELEN) how did / you...?

CHARLIE. or if you're not feeling up to it?

LUCY. i'm / feeling...

HELEN. bus. and then i / walked.

CHARLIE. it does take time. and some people take a bit longer than others.

HELEN. hello.

CHARLIE. yes?

HELEN. i'm helen. you're expecting me. you are expecting me, aren't you?

CHARLIE. i wasn't expecting anyone else.

CAL. hey. lucy.

> *they all turn to look at a man who has appeared in the kitchen. he's holding a small bunch of flowers.*

CHARLIE. oh, look here.

CAL. lucy. lucy snowe. snowy. hello. great to see you.

HELEN. lucy. we spoke, on the phone… we did speak, didn't we? i haven't been really stupid; this is the right place? i am in the right place?

CHARLIE. so if you're not ready to receive yet i can go.

LUCY. no, i mean yes.

CAL. lucy, it's cal. cal harrison.

LUCY. hi.

HELEN. i know it's supposed to be my job but i think that part of my brain just turns off after work. i'm useless at organising myself.

CHARLIE. we can postpone. if you're busy. it's not a problem. plenty of things i can be doing.

HELEN. i'm helen.

CAL. it's been a long time, hey? must be… what, ten, nearly eleven years?

CHARLIE. rearranged my day to be here and i can just rearrange it right back again.

HELEN. this is the right place?

CAL. no spring chickens any more, hey?

LUCY. really, there's no need. yes. i guess not.

CAL. oh no, i didn't mean…

    HELEN *offers her hand and they shake awkwardly.*

HELEN. lucy. how do you do?

LUCY. hi.

CAL. no, you are a spring chicken.

LUCY. thank you.

HELEN. this is unusual.

CAL. i meant me.

LUCY. thank you for coming, charlie.

CHARLIE. glad to be here, dear.

LUCY. it's good of you to come.

HELEN. oh, not at all. i've never met a... i mean, it's not often i get invited... it's nice to get out. for dinner. thank you. you're very brave.

CAL. you haven't changed at all.

CHARLIE. you're looking a bit thin, if you don't mind me saying.

LUCY. really?

CAL. it's me. i'm the old bird. the years haven't been so kind to me.

CHARLIE. cal, is it then?

CAL. hey. this is a surprise. i thought we were, i mean, i didn't realise there were, it was a...

CHARLIE. party.

CAL. no.

CHARLIE. neither did i.

they stand in silence.

LUCY. oh, i'm sorry, this is charlie.

CAL. hi.

HELEN. it's nice to meet you, charlie.

CHARLIE. likewise, i'm sure.

HELEN. i'm helen.

CHARLIE. you said.

CAL. hi there.

HELEN. hello.

they are silent again.

CAL. so. here we are.

LUCY. yes.

HELEN. how are you?

LUCY. me?

CAL. how are you feeling?

CHARLIE *hands her jacket to* LUCY.

CHARLIE. here. why don't you hang that up?

HELEN. and i brought this for you. i hope it's okay.

she gives LUCY *the wine.*

CAL. yes, sorry. these are for you.

he hands her the flowers.

LUCY. thank you. (*to* HELEN) shall i...? would you...

she hands back the wine so she can take HELEN*'s coat.*

thank you.

HELEN. thank you.

LUCY (*to* CAL). do you want...?

CAL *takes his jacket off.* LUCY *takes it, giving him the flowers back.*

CAL. thank you.

LUCY. thank you.

CAL. cheers. smells nice.

LUCY. oh f. the food.

she dumps the coats.

i'm sorry. i won't be a minute.

CHARLIE. are you struggling, dear?

HELEN. would you like some help?

CAL. do you want me to do anything?

LUCY. no, it's just / not quite…

CHARLIE. no shame in struggling.

LUCY. i can manage.

CHARLIE. perhaps you'd better let me do something.

HELEN. i'll help.

LUCY. really—

CHARLIE. it's not a problem.

LUCY. there's really no need.

CHARLIE. don't be difficult, dear.

LUCY. sorry.

HELEN. i like making myself useful.

CAL. don't you worry about anything.

the guests take over finding plates and cutlery, setting the table and assembling the meal.

LUCY. i didn't mean for you / to…

CHARLIE. what's this then?

LUCY. it's gnocchi.

CHARLIE. gnocchi?

HELEN. what's that?

CHARLIE. yes. i remember.

LUCY. it's –

CAL. italian.

LUCY. they're dumplings.

HELEN. aren't they made from potato?

CHARLIE. doesn't look like potato to me.

LUCY. no, it's –

CAL. that's not potato.

LUCY. it's semolina.

CHARLIE. semolina?

LUCY. with –

CAL. smells like goats'…

HELEN. cheese?

LUCY. yes.

CHARLIE. well, i say. (*to* CAL) you, don't just stand there, why don't you put those in a vase or something?

CAL. will do. lucy?

LUCY. er…

CAL. leave it to me.

he rummages, finds a jug and sets about stuffing the flowers into it.

CHARLIE. mind yourself.

LUCY. i'm sorry.

HELEN. plates in here?

LUCY. yes.

CHARLIE. just on the table. nothing fancy.

LUCY. that's fine, thank –

HELEN. napkins?

LUCY. er. no.

HELEN. never mind.

CHARLIE *hands* HELEN *a roll of paper towels.*

CHARLIE. here. is there any bread?

LUCY. i burnt it.

CHARLIE. home baking. ambitious.

LUCY. i'm sorry.

HELEN. never mind. glasses?

> LUCY *points to a cupboard.* CHARLIE *finds a corkscrew and takes the bottle of wine.* CAL *has finished with the flowers.*

CAL (*to* CHARLIE). shall I?

CHARLIE. think i can manage, thank you.

> *it's a screw top.*

HELEN. here, perhaps you could...

> *she hands* CAL *some candles she's found.*

CAL. oh yes. fire.

LUCY. oh, i should –

CHARLIE. don't you worry.

LUCY. there was really no need.

HELEN. we're almost there.

CAL. you sit yourself down.

CHARLIE. don't want to get in the way.

LUCY. no.

> *she sits. there's bustle around her as places are set, drinks poured and food arrives on plates.* CAL *lights some candles.*

what do i look like? what must i look like?

> *she leaves the table, finds a hand mirror, checks her reflection, smoothes her clothes. the three guests sit and wait for* LUCY *to return to the table.*

it's all here. finally. that's very kind of you.

she sits.

well, i suppose we'd better eat then.

HELEN. shall i say grace?

LUCY. what?

HELEN. grace. a few words of thanks.

CAL. oh, you're a…

HELEN. yes. if no one minds?

LUCY. no, i…

CAL. oh, please…

HELEN. if you don't –

CHARLIE. not on my behalf.

HELEN. i don't want to offend anyone.

LUCY. no. if it makes you feel… go ahead.

CHARLIE. oh.

HELEN. dear lord, thank you for this delicious food in a world where many go hungry. thank you for faith in a world of fear. and friends in a world where many people walk alone. amen.

CHARLIE. that it?

HELEN. that's it.

LUCY. thank you.

they wait. she gestures for them to start eating.

oh. please.

CAL. here we go then.

the guests eat. LUCY *stares at her plate.*

this is great, lucy.

CHARLIE. i try to eat simply as a rule.

HELEN. it's really very nice.

CHARLIE. no harm in trying something different, i suppose.

CAL. it's fantastic.

HELEN. lovely.

CAL. really tasty.

LUCY. i didn't really know what i was doing.

CHARLIE. touch-and-go, was it?

LUCY. yes. i suppose it was.

CHARLIE. only to be expected. in your condition. it's a kind of madness, you know.

CAL *raises his glass*.

CAL. cheers everyone.

they toast.

so. how do you all know each other then?

CHARLIE. oh, small talk.

CAL. how about you, helen?

HELEN. through work.

CAL. really? and what do you do? if it's not rude to ask?

HELEN. i work for the ambulance service. i'm a call handler. i take emergency calls.

CAL. a call handler?

HELEN. yes, i send the crews out.

CHARLIE. a dispenser of salvation, of course.

CAL. wow. that must be. i don't know, i don't know how it must be. i've never met one before.

HELEN. just mystery voices at the end of a line, aren't we?

CHARLIE. not any more.

HELEN. no.

CAL. and how do you / both…

CHARLIE. neighbour. aren't you hungry, lucy?

LUCY. i should probably try my own cooking, shouldn't i?

she takes a mouthful and chews.

HELEN. have you made this before?

LUCY *shakes her head.*

are you pleased?

LUCY *smiles and nods.*

oh, that's brave; isn't that brave? cooking something you
haven't made before for a dinner party. i couldn't do that.

CHARLIE. do you have many dinner parties?

HELEN. no, i don't.

CHARLIE. live alone?

HELEN. yes.

CAL. me too. but i still enjoy cooking. you must like it, lucy?

LUCY. what was that?

CAL. do you like cooking?

LUCY. i don't think so. not particularly. no.

CAL. oh.

HELEN. why's that?

LUCY. i'm not sure.

CAL. i love it.

HELEN. it's nice for a man to be able to cook.

CHARLIE. good god.

LUCY. it's the timing of things. i don't like having to deal with so many things at one time.

CAL. i quite enjoy all that. all that coordinating.

HELEN. it's satisfying, isn't it?

CHARLIE. it's self-deception, that's what.

CAL. what is?

CHARLIE. cooking. the illusion of control. that's all.

HELEN. i find it satisfying.

CHARLIE. measuring a few ingredients, twiddling a few knobs. it gives you the illusion of being in control.

CAL. interesting way of looking at it.

CHARLIE. deluding yourself. and you know why? i'll tell you why. because in life, the things that really matter, the things you really care about, you have no control over whatsoever. it all goes tits up and there's absolutely nothing you can do about it. isn't that so, lucy?

LUCY *smiles back.*

CAL. anyone been on holiday recently?

CHARLIE. no.

LUCY *and* HELEN *shake their heads.*

CAL. i went to italy a few weeks ago. to venice.

HELEN. oh, how wonderful.

CAL. only for a few days.

HELEN. venice. what a beautiful city. how nice.

CHARLIE. you've been?

HELEN. no. but i'm very interested in it. i've watched programmes about it and read about it, and i've always wanted to go. always.

CAL. it is wonderful. stunning. mind-blowing, in fact.

CHARLIE. mind-blowing?

CAL. yes, it is. you know, because i've seen the films, the
    pictures, the paintings. everybody has. everyone knows what
    it looks like, don't they? so i thought i knew what to expect.

    but really, in reality, i had no idea. seeing it for real for the
    first time, just floating there, spread out on the lagoon. i was
    completely blown away. i was, it sounds stupid perhaps, but i
    was moved.

HELEN. that doesn't sound stupid. not at all.

CAL. i got a bit emotional.

HELEN. that's wonderful.

CAL. it was.

HELEN. i'd love to go.

CAL. oh, you should.

CHARLIE. it's foolish. a folly.

CAL. sorry?

CHARLIE. there's an exercise in fear and faith for you.

HELEN. i'm sorry?

CHARLIE. venice.

HELEN. i see.

CHARLIE. built in a panic, on shit, out of fear. that's venice for
    you.

CAL. i haven't thought about it like that before.

CHARLIE. no, i expect you haven't. those first venetians, they
    were running away, weren't they? terrified. hiding from the
    hun. why else set up home on a pestilential bog? you. tell
    me, why?

CAL. er, well, i / think…

CHARLIE. simple. fear of death.

CAL (*singing*). la la la.

CHARLIE. and all those palaces and festivities and art and
    what-have-you – trumpery. just trumpery. people deluding
    themselves, distracting themselves from the horror of it all.

HELEN. the horror?

CHARLIE. disease.

CAL. maybe we / shouldn't…

CHARLIE. dying. death.

> CAL *starts coughing*.

because whatever happens…

CAL. excuse me.

HELEN. are you…?

> CHARLIE *hits him on the back*.

CAL. thanks.

CHARLIE. because whatever happens, whatever clever ideas
    people come up with, whatever desperate schemes they start,
    one day sooner or later that city's going to sink right back
    into the crap it came out of. doesn't matter how beautiful or
    mind-blowing it is.

HELEN. do you think so?

CHARLIE. that's what I think.

CAL. interesting.

HELEN. well, that's a shame. that would be such a shame. if
    there was nothing anyone could do to stop it sinking. it's a
    treasure, isn't it?

CAL. absolutely.

HELEN. precious. and so romantic.

CAL. yes.

HELEN. i've always wanted to go.

CAL. oh, i recommend it. have you been, lucy?

LUCY. no.

HELEN. who did you go with, cal?

CAL. i went on my own.

HELEN. oh, that's brave. i couldn't do that.

CHARLIE. why not?

HELEN. i'm not sure i like the idea of travelling on my own.

CAL. i used to think that.

CHARLIE. it's character-building. what are you afraid of?

HELEN. nothing. i don't know. it seems a bit extravagant
    maybe, not sharing an experience like that.

CHARLIE. you mean lonely?

CAL. you'd love it. who wouldn't?

CHARLIE. the wine please.

she is passed the bottle and tops her own glass up.

many thanks.

HELEN. i'll visit someday.

CAL. don't wait. go. and if charlie here's right then there's no
    time to waste. life's too short, you never know what's going
    to...

shit. sorry lucy.

LUCY. what?

CAL. i'm sorry for... i don't... i didn't mean to...

CHARLIE. what did he say? i missed that.

CAL. nothing.

HELEN. it was nothing.

CAL. i'm sorry.

CHARLIE. did he put his foot in it? what did he say?

HELEN. nothing.

CHARLIE. nonsense.

CAL. i wasn't thinking.

CHARLIE. spit it out.

LUCY. he just said that helen shouldn't wait to go to venice because life's too short.

CHARLIE. oh, but you're right.

CAL. thanks.

CHARLIE. he's right. it's the truth. life is short.

HELEN. you know, i don't think / lucy...

CHARLIE. no point fannying around.

CAL. look. plenty left. do you mind?

he stands up to get some more food.

CHARLIE. life is short.

CAL. would anyone else like some?

CHARLIE. shorter for some than it is for others.

CAL. maybe we should just change / the subject.

CHARLIE. and there's no consolation in thinking anything else. we know this, don't we, lucy?

LUCY. this is very... very direct, isn't it? this food, how it tastes. i didn't expect it to be so straightforward. and bright. jo's cooking's usually more... roundabout than this. softer.

HELEN. it's jo's cooking?

LUCY. his idea. his recipe.

HELEN. how nice of you to share it with us.

CHARLIE. almost biblical, helen?

LUCY. he wanted to try something different.

HELEN. you must miss him very much.

LUCY. 'miss him'?

HELEN. yes.

CAL. maybe lucy doesn't want to talk about that right now.

HELEN. of course, not if you don't want to.

CAL. maybe now's not the time.

HELEN. but if you'd like to?

LUCY. i don't know if i can.

HELEN. it's good to talk about these things, isn't it?

CHARLIE. and you'd know, would you?

HELEN. actually i've done training / in...

CHARLIE. has it happened to you?

HELEN. not as such, no.

CHARLIE. well, then.

CAL. so maybe we should move on.

HELEN. but it helps. sharing.

CHARLIE. rubbish.

HELEN. it's healthy.

CHARLIE. it's got nothing to do with health. it's about
    survival. some things you have to bury to survive. why do
    you people think it's good to talk about what is painful?
    dredge it all up again.

HELEN. so we know we're not alone.

CHARLIE. listen, dear, we come into this world alone and we go out alone. that's life.

HELEN. that's a very sad way of looking at it.

CHARLIE. it's realistic, that's all.

HELEN. no one need be on their own, charlie.

CHARLIE. so you hope.

HELEN. so i trust. believe.

CHARLIE. trust? belief? what are they worth?

HELEN. everything. they sustain us.

CHARLIE. no use to you when the shit really hits the fan.

HELEN. no, they help us make sense of the sh... world. otherwise, what's the point?

CHARLIE. i thought you lot were supposed to have the answers. you tell me.

CAL *comes back to the table and picks up the wine bottle.*

CAL. this is stimulating. more wine anyone? lucy?

LUCY. i don't get it.

HELEN. what was that?

LUCY. i don't get it.

CHARLIE. don't blame you, dear. neither do i.

CAL. yeah. life, hey?

LUCY. i don't get what happened.

CAL. when?

LUCY. one day, one minute we're here. an ordinary day. and then everything changes. everything. how did it happen?

CAL. jo? shit. sorry.

LUCY. can i say this? is this okay?

CAL. are you / asking…

HELEN. you go ahead.

CHARLIE. your house, you say whatever you want.

LUCY. one minute, there's jo, there's me. the two of us. we're here and we know what we're doing. he knows what we're doing. but then everything changes and i don't recognise anything any more. what happened?

HELEN. a terrible thing, lucy.

LUCY. i'm a logical person. i'm a rational person.

CHARLIE. there's no plan, no pattern, dear.

LUCY. but charlie, i can go back and look. i can see (*she indicates her head*) here. here we are. me and jo. one picture of us after another, one feeling of us after another. days and weeks and years of them. and they all connect and everything is clear.

or that's what i thought. what did i get wrong?

HELEN. nothing, nothing at all.

LUCY. but then what happens when i turn around, what happens then is… is not the logical outcome of everything that goes before it. it makes no sense.

CHARLIE. it doesn't, dear. it won't ever.

LUCY. jo would have said if he didn't feel well. and he didn't. he didn't say anything about not feeling well.

HELEN. these haemorrhages, 'events' the medics call them, these events, lucy, sometimes they can happen without warning.

LUCY. but that's no good. that's no use to me. that's not what i need to know.

she gets up from the table.

okay. look, i'm here. jo's here. we're cooking this, exactly this meal. we're talking. i'm facing this way. i bend down. there's a noise. something hits the floor. jo has dropped something.

i turn. i see him. he's dropped a spoon. he goes to kneel down. sits down on the floor here. i say, 'jo, what are you doing?'

what time is it?

CAL. it's just gone nine fifteen.

LUCY. no, that's not it. helen. what time did i call you? when did i ask for help?

HELEN. your call was put through at 19:20.

LUCY. twenty past seven.

so it's, what, maybe a couple of minutes before, maybe seventeen, maybe eighteen minutes past when i tell him to stop messing around? he's making these strange animal noises. actually, what i say is 'stop it, jo. stop fucking about.' that's what i say. 'stop fucking about.' what a stupid thing to say.

CAL. how were you to know?

LUCY. yes. how was i supposed to know? what time did the ambulance come, helen?

HELEN. twenty-nine minutes past.

LUCY. when it came there were two of them. two men. and they did things to jo lying there on the floor. they talked to me, tried talking to jo. what did they say? do you know?

HELEN. i don't know for sure but i think they would've explained what they were doing and what was happening. they would've asked him questions and asked him to respond.

LUCY. but he didn't. he couldn't. and then they put him on a stretcher and they took him away.

CHARLIE. you went with them, lucy. i saw you go with them.

LUCY. yes, i did. i went with them. i called you at twenty past seven and the ambulance arrived nine minutes later?

HELEN. yes.

LUCY. nine minutes. and he was still mine. tell me, helen. what happened?

HELEN. i'm not sure i know what you want me to say.

LUCY. those nine minutes. you stayed on the phone, didn't you? you asked me things. you told me what to do.

HELEN. you answered my questions. you told me what we needed to know about jo's condition. they're standard questions. there's a script i have to follow.

LUCY. you asked me if he was agitated or aggressive. you asked me if i thought he could understand me, if he could speak. yes?

HELEN. yes.

LUCY. you said i should see if he could squeeze my hand.

HELEN. yes.

LUCY. you asked me if i thought he was finding it hard to breathe. you said to look at the colour of his lips.

and you told me to keep talking to him. 'talk to jo; he can hear you.' even though he couldn't move or speak.

and i did?

HELEN. yes, i think so.

LUCY. you think so?

HELEN. i'm sure you did.

LUCY. nine minutes.

i had his hand. i held his hand. i said... what?

i can see his hand in mine. and i can feel us. and my lips are moving but i can't hear the words. i'm babbling. saying nothing. saying everything's going to be just fine.

you told me to keep talking to him because your hearing is the last thing to go, isn't it? when you're dying?

HELEN *nods*.

yes, i knew that. i'd heard that before somewhere. that's why i kept talking. because he was leaving me.

i swore at him.

CHARLIE. that's understandable, / dear.

LUCY. i wanted to be good and say the best for us both. tell him what he needed to hear. i wanted to explain myself.

i said i was sorry for being obtuse, for being difficult. i never meant to be. i don't mean to be. i want to be clear and pure and straight.

i should've said more. i wish i'd… i tried… this is really fucking hard.

i said 'jo, listen. listen to this.' i said 'jo, i've kept what you've told me. it's here. always.

i know only ever to use the freshest eggs for poaching. i know that hot milk makes your mashed potato fluffy. i know that a warm bowl makes for a better sponge.

i know that i've been loved. i know what you know. please know how much i love you.'

that's it. god, is that it?

HELEN. i'm sure it's what he needed to hear, lucy.

LUCY. don't say that. you don't know. you can't. only jo can say.

and he won't because he's not coming back. because he's dead. jo is dead.

you asked me how i am. well, i can tell you. i can tell you how i feel, cal.

CAL. oh, you don't… it was a dumb question.

LUCY. no, i want to. really. i feel full of sadness. full of it. heavy with it. and at the same time, i feel like i've been emptied out. dug out like a big hole.

isn't that strange? isn't it strange that jo's not being here is so big, so massive, that it is here? it's absolutely this. now.

there. this probably wasn't the kind of evening you were hoping for.

CAL. hey, no problem.

CHARLIE. i wasn't expecting much, dear.

HELEN. no, i'm having a lovely time.

LUCY. it's okay. it's fine, isn't it? all fine. because here we are safe and well. and on we go.

has everyone finished?

they nod.

then i'll clear this away.

she gets up and takes a few dishes over to the sink.

if you want to go, then please… there's really not much to hang around for.

CHARLIE. is that it?

HELEN. i'm in no hurry, lucy. don't worry about me.

CAL. are we done then?

LUCY. i did make a pudding.

CAL. great.

LUCY. but i doubt it's any good.

HELEN. i'm sure it'll be lovely.

CHARLIE. my appetite's not what it was. but seeing as i'm here...

LUCY. you want to try it?

HELEN. only if it's no trouble, if you want to stop...

CAL. in for a penny...

CHARLIE. not if you're not up to it...

LUCY. let's have pudding.

CAL. okay.

HELEN. well, let me / help...

LUCY. no, please. i can manage. you sit there.

> *the guests sit in silence.* LUCY *stacks the plates, takes them away and returns to the table with pudding. she puts it on the table and goes away again to get bowls and spoons.*

CAL. wow.

HELEN. what is it?

CHARLIE. it's moving.

LUCY. it's blancmange. i hope. (*she sits*) thank you for coming. i do appreciate it. thank you.

CHARLIE. no need to thank anybody.

LUCY. there is, charlie. especially you. charlie's been very kind to me.

CAL. yes?

CHARLIE. it's not kindness. it's common sense.

LUCY. no, kindness. that's what it feels like to me. charlie lives next door. she's been leaving food for me since jo died.

HELEN. that is kind.

CHARLIE. nothing fancy.

CAL. i imagine not.

CHARLIE. fuel. that's all. it's such an effort to keep going… in grief.

LUCY. blancmange, helen?

HELEN. a tiny bit, please.

CHARLIE. you don't want to have to think about yourself when this happens to you. you can't. not in all the confusion.

LUCY. no.

HELEN. thank you.

LUCY. charlie?

CHARLIE. oh, alright then. it's too boring. mundane. that's the word.

LUCY. cal?

CAL. yes, please.

CHARLIE. too mundane to bother about. that's how i felt when my sweetie died. she liked venice.

LUCY. charlie. i didn't know.

CHARLIE. and why should you? it was years ago.

LUCY. i'm so sorry.

CHARLIE. don't be. i'm not sorry for me. i choose to endure, i don't have to. no one's forcing me to. and besides, there are always new people to meet. there's always fun to be had.

LUCY. thank you, charlie. thank you for thinking for me.

CHARLIE. that's all right, dear.

LUCY *finishes serving herself.*

LUCY. maybe it tastes okay.

they all try it.

CAL. wow.

HELEN. lucy, it's lovely.

CHARLIE. interesting texture.

LUCY. i was worried it looked like cum at one stage.

HELEN. oh.

CHARLIE. i wouldn't know, dear.

LUCY. jo was right. it's fine.

CAL. more than fine.

LUCY. delicious. yes.

they eat.

CHARLIE. so who did you say you are?

CAL. me?

CHARLIE. yes, you.

CAL. i knew lucy from before.

CHARLIE. before what?

LUCY. jo. cal and i were at college together.

CHARLIE. i see.

HELEN. how nice.

CAL. oh, nothing like that...

LUCY. oh god no.

they quickly finish the blancmange appreciatively.

that's it, i'm afraid. i've nothing left to offer you. no coffee, or cheese, or brandy... i hope you've had enough. it's been a funny old evening, i guess.

CHARLIE. as dinner parties go...

CAL. the food was great though. and the company. everything. great.

HELEN. thank you very much for inviting me, lucy.

LUCY. i'm grateful you came. you didn't have to.

HELEN. i wanted to, i did really. all those people i talk to in my job and never see. you can feel so far away.

CHARLIE. don't you need a hand clearing up, dear?

HELEN. oh yes, / let me...

LUCY. no, thank you. both of you. you've done enough.

HELEN. i really don't mind. i'm in no rush.

LUCY. i think i've had as much fun as i can take for one evening.

HELEN. well, if it's what you want.

CHARLIE. time to go?

LUCY. i'm very tired.

HELEN. what about all this?

LUCY. it's not so bad.

CHARLIE. well, if that's what lucy wants.

LUCY. yes, please. you go on home.

HELEN. righty-ho then. shall i...

    LUCY *hands them their coats.*

    thank you.

CHARLIE. soup tomorrow, dear?

LUCY. it's okay, charlie. i'll take it from here.

CHARLIE. good girl.

CAL. i guess it's time to hit the road then.

LUCY. hang on, cal. have you got a minute?

CAL. sure.

CHARLIE. oh, i see. (*to* HELEN) we'd best be going.

HELEN. yes, okay. well, goodbye then.

CAL. nice to meet you, helen.

HELEN. lovely to meet you too.

CAL. don't forget venice now.

HELEN. we'll always have venice. bye then. goodbye lucy. thank you so much for having me.

LUCY. thank you, helen.

CAL. bye then.

HELEN. bye.

CHARLIE. and charmed to meet you too.

CAL. yes, sorry, bye charlie.

LUCY. goodnight.

HELEN. god bless.

CHARLIE. oh please.

　　CHARLIE *and* HELEN *leave*.

CAL. interesting woman.

LUCY. which one?

CAL. you're sure i can't give you a hand here, lucy?

LUCY. no, it's fine. really. i'd rather do it myself.

CAL. would you like me to take the rubbish out or something?

LUCY. no. nothing like that.

CAL. okay.

LUCY. tell me, cal. what did i use to be like? all those years ago?

CAL. at college?

LUCY. yes. before i knew jo. what was i like?

CAL. what did you look like?

LUCY. no. i mean, who was i?

CAL. gosh. that's quite a question. i don't know, lucy. tough question.

LUCY. i guess.

CAL. i don't know what to say. you used to smoke. how's that?

LUCY. that much i remember.

CAL. that's a tough question, you know. blimey.

LUCY. i'm sorry. it's stupid to ask. i'm sorry.

CAL. no, no.

LUCY. no, really. forget it. please. how can you possibly answer that?

CAL. life, hey?

LUCY. it's about things disappearing.

CAL. like venice?

LUCY. i didn't realise. but now i know.

CAL. i haven't been much help to you, have i?

LUCY. hard to tell.

CAL. is that why you invited me? to ask me that question?

LUCY. i guess. is that weird?

CAL. no, no. i mean, it was a surprise to hear from you, yes. but no, no. perfectly normal, i expect. given the circumstances.

LUCY. are you on your own?

CAL. single? oh yes.

LUCY. for a long time? you don't have to say if you don't want to.

CAL. no, it's okay. i don't mind. it's been a few years now. five. six.

LUCY. and how is it?

CAL. it's what i'm used to, i suppose. it's just fine. i've got friends, work, a roof over my head. i'm pretty happy, all things considered.

LUCY. you don't want anyone?

CAL. well, maybe, one day. you know, if the right woman comes along.

so maybe, i should…

LUCY. yes.

CAL goes to get his jacket. LUCY goes to a drawer, takes an address book out and copies something onto a scrap of paper.

here.

CAL. what's this?

he takes the paper from her.

LUCY. helen's number. she fancies you.

CAL. right. gosh. really?

LUCY. definitely.

CAL. shit. i mean good. yes. thank you. are you going to be okay? on your own?

LUCY. on my own? i don't think i'll ever be on my own again, cal. there are ghosts here.

CAL. oh god –

LUCY. no, joking. don't worry. i'm fine. you make sure you call helen.

CAL. i will.

LUCY. and let me know how it goes.

CAL. sure, sure. well, if you need anything, you know where i am.

LUCY. yes.

CAL. i mean it. anything at all. give me a call.

LUCY. okay.

CAL. i'll be seeing you then, hey?

he kisses her awkwardly on the cheek.

LUCY. yes, see you again, cal.

CAL. cheers, lucy. look after yourself. (*indicating the phone number*) and thanks.

LUCY. bye.

he leaves.

LUCY *is alone. she puts some music on then clears the table, leaving only the lit candles. she sits down and finishes the wine in her glass. she blows the candles out.*

the end.

Recipes for *What We Know*

by Rosie Sykes

Rosie Sykes has cooked in the kitchens of some of Britain's most celebrated chefs including Joyce Molyneux, Shaun Hill and Alastair Little. In 2001 she set up and ran a critically acclaimed gastro pub – The Sutton Arms in Smithfield, London. Between 2001 and 2003 she contributed regular features to the Guardian's Weekend *magazine, as the Kitchen Doctor. Rosie's approach to food and cooking is simple but uncompromising. As a talented and passionate gardener she is committed to making the best of local and seasonal ingredients. Rosie combines a keen interest in food history and culture with an intuitive understanding of food and cooking. She is co-author of* The Kitchen Revolution (*Ebury Press, 2008*).

Goats' cheese and semolina gnocchi with puttanesca sauce

The puttanesca sauce that accompanies the gnocchi is unctuous, sweet, sour and ever so slightly chillified. Puttanesca is Italian for prostitute so this sauce, as the name suggests, is not supposed to be subtle – big, brassy flavours are what's required. You can make it without the bacon if you wish.

Ingredients for the gnocchi
Flavourless oil
375ml milk
Nutmeg
125g semolina
30g parmesan
1 egg
200g goats' cheese
Salt and pepper

Ingredients for the puttanesca sauce
200g pancetta or smoked back bacon
2 medium onions
2 tbsp olive oil
2 cloves garlic
1 red chilli
1.5 tbsp sherry or white wine vinegar
2 x 410g tins of peeled tomatoes
2 tbsp tomato paste
5-6 stalks thyme
1 bay leaf
50g capers
75g stoned black olives
Pinch of sugar
Parmesan
Salt and pepper

Things you can do if you have any spare moments prior to starting to cook:
Peel and slice the onions and garlic. Deseed and finely chop the chilli.

1 hour 20 minutes before you want to eat:
Preheat the oven to 180/350/gas4. Boil a kettle and find a large, ovenproof dish approx 30cm x 15cm x 5cm that will fit inside a roasting tin. Grease the dish with flavourless oil.

Next, make the gnocchi. Put the milk in a saucepan with a grating of nutmeg and a good dose of seasoning. Pour in the semolina and bring it up to the boil over a medium heat, stirring constantly. Carry on stirring until the mixture has become almost solid then take it off the heat and beat in the eggs and parmesan.

Pour half of the mixture into the large dish, cover it with goats' cheese. Depending on what type of goats' cheese you have got, either crumble it or slice it and distribute it over the gnocchi, add some seasoning and then spread with the rest of the semolina. Cover the dish with a couple of butter papers or some lightly oiled parchment and seal with some foil. Put the dish with the gnocchi inside a roasting tin and pour boiling water halfway up the tin. Place in the oven and bake the gnocchi for 25-30 minutes.

While the gnocchi is in the oven, make the tomato sauce. Using a pair of scissors, snip the pancetta or bacon into 2cm pieces, straight into a large, heavy-based pan and fry over a medium heat until it starts to brown and let off some of its fat. While the bacon is cooking, peel and finely slice the onions. Once browned lift the bacon out with a slotted spoon and put it to one side. Add a splash of olive oil to the pan and cook the onions for about 10 minutes until very soft and starting to brown. Meanwhile, peel and slice the garlic. Deseed and finely chop the chilli. When the onion has been cooking for 10 minutes, add the garlic, fry for a couple of minutes then add the chilli. Turn the heat up, stir them about for another couple of minutes, and then splash in the vinegar. Use a wooden spoon to scrape the bottom of the pan and cook until the vinegar has all but disappeared. Then add the tomatoes, along with the bacon, the tomato paste, the thyme leaves stripped from their thick stalks, the bay leaf, the olives and the capers, and some seasoning. Stir well, bring to the boil then allow to simmer on a low heat uncovered for at least 50 minutes or until the liquid has reduced to a thick sauce.

Once the gnocchi is cooked, take it out and leave to cool for at least 20 minutes or until it is completely cold. Turn the oven right down at this point. When the gnocchi is cold, cut it into portion-size squares or triangles.

Heat a good splash of oil in a large frying pan and add the four pieces of gnocchi. Let them cook until they are browned thoroughly on the bottom then turn them over and brown them on the other side - it will take about 5 minutes on each side. Keep the gnocchi in a low oven while you cook the rest.

Serve the gnocchi with the rich tomato sauce and an extra grating of parmesan.

Blancmange

A lovely wobbly jelly pudding.

Ingredients
500ml milk
540ml double cream
1 vanilla pod
60g sugar
4 leaves gelatine
1 measure grappa

To serve
Fruit

4 hours before you want to eat:
Put the cream, sugar and half the milk into a saucepan. Split the vanilla pod in half and scrape the seeds into the pan and bring the mixture up to a boil. When it has boiled, take it off the heat. Put the rest of the milk into a bowl and add the gelatine leaves. Push the leaves under the liquid and allow to soak for about 5 minutes until completely softened. Use your hands to pick up the gelatine, hold it over the bowl in which it was soaking and give it a good squeeze to remove any excess liquid. Set the liquid it softened in to one side.

Stir the softened gelatine into the hot milk and cream until it has completely dissolved then tip this into the other liquid. Stir well and leave to cool. Set it over iced water to aid the cooling and setting.

When the blancmange starts to set, pour into individual moulds or cups, something from which it can be turned out. Place them in the fridge until set.

Once set, dip each mould or cup in boiling water to loosen the blancmange and turn them out onto individual plates.

A Nick Hern Book

What We Know first published in Great Britain as a paperback original in 2010 by Nick Hern Books Limited, The Glasshouse, 49a Goldhawk Road, London W12 8QP, in association with the Traverse Theatre, Edinburgh

Reprinted 2016

What We Know copyright © 2010 Pamela Carter

Pamela Carter has asserted her right to be identified as the author of this work

Cover photograph: Laurence Winram with Kate Dickie as Lucy
Cover design: Ned Hoste, 2H

Typeset by Nick Hern Books, London
Printed in the UK by Mimeo Ltd, Huntingdon, Cambridgeshire PE29 6XX

A CIP catalogue record for this book is available from the British Library

ISBN   978 1 84842 092 2

Short Circular Walks

in

WEST YORKSHIRE

by John N. Merrill

Maps, sketches and photographs by John N. Merrill

"I hike the paths and trails of the world for others to enjoy."

© *John N. Merrill 2003.*

Walk & Write Ltd.

The Short Circular Walks Series.

2003

Walk & Write Ltd.,
Marathon House,
Longcliffe, Nr. Matlock,
Derbyshire, England. DE4 4HN

Tel/Fax 01629 - 540991
email - marathonhiker@aol.com

Typset and designed by John N. Merrill & Walk & Write Ltd.
Printed and handmade by John N. Merrill.

©
©Text - - John N. Merrill. 2002.
  Photographs, Maps & sketches - John N. Merrill. 2002

ISBN 0-9-7496-91-1
First published - Janyaru 1992.
Revised and reprinted - November 2002

British Library Cataloguing-in-Publication Data. A catalogue record of this book is available from the British Library.

Typeset in Bookman - bold, italic, and plain 10pt, 14pt and 18pt .

Please note - The maps in this guide are purely illustrative. You are encouraged to use the appropriate 1:25,000 O.S. map.

John Merrill has walked all the routes in this book. Meticulous research has been undertaken to ensure that this publication is highly accurate at the time of going to press. The publishers, however, cannot be held responsible for alterations, errors omissions, or for changes in details given. They would welcome inform to help keep the book up to date.

Cover design - by John N. Merrill - Walk & Write Ltd 2002
Cover photograph - Cobbled path from Upper Denby to Denby Dale, by John N. Merrill.

CONTENTS

Few people have walked the earth's crust more than John Merrill with more than 178,000 miles in the last 32 years - the average person walks 75,000 miles in a lifetime. Apart from walking too much causing bones in his feet to snap, like metal fatigue, he has never suffered from any back, hip or knee problems. Like other walkers he has suffered from many blisters, his record is 23 on both feet! He wears out at least three pairs of boots a year and his major walking has cost over £125,000. This includes 95 pairs of boots costing more than £11,600 and over £1,800 on socks - a pair of socks last three weeks and are not washed!

His marathon walks in Britain include - -

Hebridean Journey....... 1,003 miles. Northern Isles Journey......913 miles.
Irish Island Journey ....1,578 miles.   Parkland Journey.......2,043 miles.
Land's End to John o' Groats.....1,608 miles.
The East of England Heritage Route - 450miles.

and in 1978 he became the first person to walk the entire coastline of Britain - 6,824 miles in ten months.

In Europe he has walked across Austria - 712 miles - hiked the Tour of Mont Blanc, the Normandy coast, the Loire Valley (450 miles), a high level route across the Augverne(230 miles) and the River Seine (200 miles) in France, completed High Level Routes in the Dolomites and Italian Alps, and the GR20 route across Corsica in training! Climbed the Tatra Mountains ,the Transylvanian Alps in Romania, and in Germany walked in the Taunus, Rhine, the Black Forest (Clock Carriers Way) and King Ludwig Way (Bavaria). He has walked across Europe - 2,806 miles in 107 days - crossing seven countries, the Swiss and French Alps and the complete Pyrennean chain - the hardest and longest mountain walk in Europe, with more than 600,000 feet of ascent! In 1998 he walked 1,100 miles along the pilgrimage route from Le Puy (France) to Santiago (Spain) and onto Cape Finisterre; in 2002 walked 700 miles from Seville to Santiago de Compostela.

In America he used The Appalachian Trail - 2,200 miles - as a training walk, before walking from Mexico to Canada via the Pacific Crest Trail in record time - 118 days for 2,700 miles. Recently he walked most of the Continental Divide Trail and much of New Mexico; his second home. In 1999 he walked the Chesopeake & Ohio Canal National Historical Trail. In 2,000 he became the first thru hiker to walk 1,340 miles around Ohio, following the Buckeye Trail. In Canada he has walked the Rideau Trail - Kingston to Ottowa - 220 miles and The Bruce Trail - Tobermory to Niagara Falls - 460 miles.

In 1984 John set off from Virginia Beach on the Atlantic coast, and walked 4,226 miles without a rest day, across the width of America to Santa Cruz and San Francisco on the Pacific coast. His walk is unquestionably his greatest achievement, being, in modern history, the longest, hardest crossing of the U.S.A. in the shortest time - under six months (178 days). The direct distance is 2,800 miles.

Between major walks John is out training in his own area - The Peak District National Park. He has walked all of our National Trails many times - The Cleveland Way thirteen times and The Pennine Way four times in a year! He has been trekking in the Himalayas five times. He created more than thirty-five challenge walks which have been used to raise more than £600,000 for charity. From his own walks he has raised over £100,000. He is author of more than 220 walking guides which he prints and publishes himself, His book sales are in excess of 3 million, He has created many long distance walks including The Limey Way, The Peakland Way, Dark Peak Challenge walk, Rivers' Way, The Belvoir Witches Challenge Walk, The Forest of Bowland Challenge. the Dore to New Mills Challenge Walk , the Lincolnshire Wolds "Black Death" Challenge Walk and the Happy Hiker (White Peak) Challenge Walk. His new Pilgrim Walk Series includes the 72 mile, "Walsingham Way" - Ely to Walsingham. His monthly walks appear in Derbyshire's "Reflections" magazine. In January 2003, he was honoured for his walking and writing, recieving a Honorary degree, Master of the University, from Derby University.

4

INTRODUCTION

My school days were spent in Harrogate and my father always drove me to boarding school, each term. Our route from Sheffield took us through Wakefield and I soon became familiar with Newmillerdam, Ackworth and Ferrybridge. I never envisaged it would be so long before I would exploring these area's on foot. The Huddersfield area I was familiar with but again, although I travelled through frequently, it was several years before I walked here. Earlier books have explored the Peak District and South Yorkshire, so it was a logical progression to move northwards. For the purposes of this book I have purposefully restricted myself to the Pontefract, Wakefield and Huddersfield area. The rest of West Yorkshire I have left for another book!

My aim has been to get an even spread over the region while attempting to cover as much diverse walking as possible. The scope is endless. The Ferrybridge walk is mostly outside West Yorkshire but a fascinating area to explore. Ackworth and Badsworth walks are a delight and very attractive villages steeped in history. The line of the old Barnsley Canal walk in Haw Park is still one of my favourite canal walks and exceptionally attractive. The walk around Horbury Cut is also exceptional although the canal here is much wider. I had to include Newmillerdam and Bretton Park, if just out of sentiment, but realistically they are both excellent walks.

The walks in the Huddersfield area are most attractive with the Narrow Canal walk a must. Holmfirth is fascinating and the walk takes you into the high country, as does the one on Marsden Moor; one of the longest but rewarding walks in the book. Denby Dale has much to offer and I could have done four walks here. The one around Gunthwaite remains as one of the finest short walks I have ever done. Castle Hill walk is a stunning vantage point and the Mag Dale walk is in a wooded valley well worth exploring.

Here then are sixteen walks in West Yorkshire - some hard, some easy - but illustrating the variety of the area. I have derived many hours of pleasure exploring the byways of West Yorkshire and I hope they give you equally as much pleasure.

Happy Walking!
John N. Merrill

Whilst every care is taken detailing and describing the walk in this book, it should be borne in mind that the countryside changes by the seasons and the work of man. I have described the walk to the best of my ability, detailing what I have found on the walk in the way of stiles and signs. Obviously with the passage of time stiles become broken or replaced by a ladder stile or even a small gate. Signs too have a habit of being broken or pushed over. All the route follow rights of way and only on rare occasions will you have to overcome obstacles in its path, such as a barbed wire fence or electric fence. On rare occasions rights of way are rerouted and these ammendments are included in the next edition.

The seasons bring occasional problems whilst out walking which should also be borne in mind. In the height of summer paths become overgrown and you will have to fight your way through in a few places. In low lying areas the fields are often full of crops, and although the pathline goes straight across it may be more practical to walk round the field edge to get to the next stile or gate. In summer the ground is generally dry but in autumn and winter, especially because of our climate, the surface can be decidedly wet and slippery; sometimes even gluttonous mud!

These comments are part of countryside walking which help to make your walk more interesting or briefly frustrating. Standing in a farmyard up to your ankles in mud might not be funny at the time but upon reflection was one of the highlights of the walk!

The mileage for each section is based on three calculations -

1. pedometer reading.
2. the route map measured on the map.
3. the time I took for the walk.

I believe the figure stated for each section to be very accurate but we all walk differently and not always in a straight line! The time allowed for each section is on the generous side and does not include pub stops etc. The figure is based on the fact that on average a person walks 2 1/2 miles an hours but less in hilly terrain.

EQUIPMENT NOTES by John N. Merrill

Today there is a bewildering variety of walking gear, much is superfluous to general walking in Britain. As a basic observation, people over dress for the outdoors. Basically equipment should be serviceable and do the task. I don't approve of walking poles; humans were built to walk with two legs! The following are some of my throughts.

BOOTS - For summer use and day walking I wear lightweight boots. For high mountains and longer trips I prefer a good quality boot with a full leather upper, of medium weight, with a vibram sole. I always add a foam cushioned insole to help cushion the base of my feet.

SOCKS - I generally wear two thick pairs as this helps minimise blisters. The inner pair are of loop stitch variety and approximately 80% wool. The outer are a thick rib pair of approximately 80% wool.

CLOTHES & WATERPROOFS - for general walking I wear a T shirt or cotton shirt with a cotton wind jacket on top, and shorts - even in snow! You generate heat as you walk and I prefer to layer my clothes to avoid getting too hot. Depending on the season will dictate how many layers you wear. In soft rain I just use my wind jacket for I know it quickly dries out. In heavy or consistant rain I slip on a poncho, which covers my pack and allows air to circulate, while keeping dry. Only in extreme conditions will I don overtrousers, much preferring to get wet and feel comfortable. I never wear gaiters!

FOOD - as I walk I carry bars of chocolate, for they provide instant energy and are light to carry. In winter a flask of hot coffee is welcome. I never carry water and find no hardship from not doing so, but this is a personal matter! From experience I find the more I drink the more I want and sweat. You should always carry some extra food such as trail mix & candy bars etc., for emergencies.

RUCKSACKS - for day walking I use a climbing rucksack of about 40 litre capacity and although it leaves excess space it does mean that the sac is well padded, with an internal frame and padded shoulder straps. Inside apart from the basics for one day in winter I carry gloves, balaclava, spare pullover and a pair of socks.

MAP & COMPASS - when I am walking I always have the relevant map - preferably 1:25,000 scale - open in my hand. This enables me to constantly check that I am walking the right way. In case of bad weather I carry a compass, which once mastered gives you complete confidence in thick cloud or mist.

FERRYBRIDGE - 3 MILES

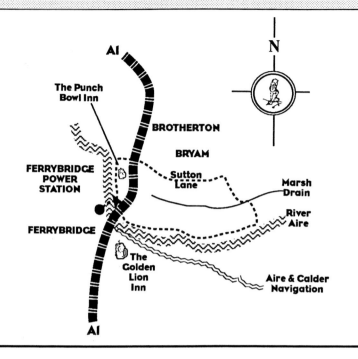

WALKING INSTRUCTIONS - Cross the stone Toll Bridge over the River Aire and turn left and descend a well defined path to a stile. Just after gain the banks of the River Aire and for the next 1/2 mile keep the river on your left. Ascend a stile by a footpath sign and reach the road in Brotherton. Bear left along it and in a few yards pass the Punch Bowl Inn on your right. Just after and before the railway bridge, turn right up a tarmaced path and follow it into woodland. Upon meeting another tarmaced path turn right along it and soon cross a large footbridge over the A1. Shortly afterwards reach a main road. Cross to your right to Sutton Lane and walk along this for the next 3/4 mile. First passing houses, then an open lane until Old Barn on your right and Village Farm on your left. Here turn right, as footpath signed, and walk along Marsh Lane. The lane curves left them right to the top of Marsh Drain. Here keep straight ahead and cross the field of Brotherton Marsh, aiming for the prominent church tower on the otherside of the River Aire. In 1/4 mile reach the banks of the river and turn right. For more than a mile walk along the banks of the river with views of the Aire & Calder Navigation and Golden Lion Inn. After a mile bear right to the kissing gate underneath the A1 flyover. Here turn left and recross the toll bridge back to your starting point.

FERRYBRIDGE
- 3 MILES
- allow 1 1/4 hours.

 *- Toll Bridge, Ferrybridge - River Aire - Brotherton - Bryam - Marsh Lane - Marsh Drain - Brotherton Marsh - River Aire - Toll Bridge, Ferrybridge.*

 - 1:25,000 Explorer Series No. 289 - Leeds.

and start *- Layby close to old Toll Bridge in Ferrybridge on the B6136 road near entrance to Ferrybridge Power Station. Grid Ref. SE483246.*

- Punch Bowl Inn, Brotherton; The Golden Lion Inn beside start of Aire & Calder Navigation, 100 yards from start of walk.

ABOUT THE WALK - Ferrybridge on the boundary of West Yorkshire has always been a busy place with the Great North Road (A1) and its power station. The loading of coal from the barges into the power station was a fascinating scene of a bygone era. I wanted to explore the area and the start of the Aire & Calder Navigation but unless doing an end to end walk a circular walk within the boundaries of West Yorkshire was not practical. Therefore, you start in West Yorkshire but cross the River Aire by the impressive toll bridge, built in 1804, and walk in North Yorkshire beside the Aire but with views of the navigation. A very enjoyable short walk seeing the spectrum of travel over the decades.

AIRE & CALDER NAVIGATION - Connects Wakefield via Castleford to Goole and since the beginning the 18th century has been a busy and prosperous route to a sea port. The Ferrybridge Power Station, on the River Aire, used to have daily deliveries of coal - as much as 1 1/2 million tons a year. If time permits a visit to the Ferrybridge Pottery (Royal Cauldon Pottery), on Pottery Lane, is worth visiting to see how fine earthenware has been made here since 1793.

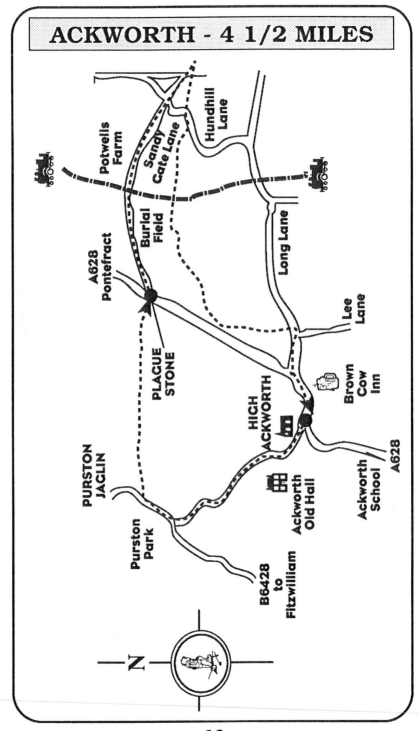

ACKWORTH
- 4 1/2 MILES
- allow 1 3/4 hours.

- High Ackworth - Purston Lane - Purston Park - Purston Jaglin - Castle Syke Hill - Plague Stone - Hundhill - Burial Field - High Ackworth.

- 1:25,000 Explorer Series No. 278 - Sheffield & Barnsley.

& START - No official one but roadside parking beside triangle and cross at High Ackworth. Grid Reference SE441179.

- Brown Cow, High Ackworth.

ABOUT THE WALK - Ackworth is particularly attractive village full of interesting buildings and associations to the plague that was prevalent here in 1645. This walk takes you to a few of the places associated with its past and is half lane and path walking. The walk can also be used as an extension to the Badsworth walk. Ackworth is renowned for its Quaker School which dates back to 1779.

WALKING INSTRUCTIONS - Starting from the triangle close to the Brown Cow Inn and drive to church turn left out of the top of the triangle along Purston Lane (B6421 road.) The lane has a footpath and once round the first corner on your left is the impressive Ackworth Old Hall. Keep on the lane for the next mile to the road junction with the B6428 road. Turn right towards Purston Jaglin and in 1/4 mile opposite the path entrance into Purston Park turn right onto a track passing house No. 103 almost immediately. Keep on this track for the next 1 1/4 miles as you gently meander and ascend gently to the A628 road at Castle Syke Hill. Turn right then left along Sandy Gate Lane. Here at the road junction is the plaque and Plague Stone. When the plague ravished here money was left in the hollow on top in vinegar water, in return for food.

Follow Sandy Gate Lane round and down and over the railway line. Just after pass Potwells Farm on your left. 1/4 mile later reach a small cross roads. Continue ahead with the wall on Hundhill Hall on your

right. In 100 yards turn right over the stone stile by the path sign and cross the field edge to another stone stile and path sign - on your right is Hundhill Hall. Turn left along Hundhill Lane and in 30 yards turn right to a stile and path sign. The pathline keeps close to the righthand field edge before following round to your left to a bridge over the railway. Over this continue straight ahead to a stile. Continue straight ahead across the next field to its perimeter where turn left and follow the field edge down and round to a path sign. The field to your right is the Burial Field. Just after the path sign you keep the field edge on your left as you keep straight ahead across two fields and two wooden footbridges. Continue across the third field to a path sign above the A628 road. You can descend to the road and follow it back to the Brown Cow Inn, but instead turn left and follow the defined path across the field to the lefthand side of a solitary bungalow (Brookfield). Here gain a stile, footpath sign and road. Turn right and in a few yards reach the road junction with the A628 road beside an impressive road sign dated 1827. Turn left to the Brown Cow Inn and triangle where you began.

Ackworth Old Hall.

Ferrybridge bridge built in 1804.

BADSWORTH - 5 MILES

Lee Lane

Ackworth School

Low Ackworth

Tan House Lane

Low Farm

Burnhill Bridge

Track – Stone flagged

Moor House

Rockingham Corse

Burnhill Lane

Ninevah Farm

Ninevah Lane

Badsworth Hall

Owler's Lane

St. Mary's

Rogerthorpe Manor

New Road

N

BADSWORTH

to UPTON

BADSWORTH
- 5 MILES
- allow 2 hours.

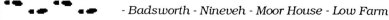 *- Badsworth - Nineveh - Moor House - Low Farm - Low Ackworth - Tan House Dike - Burnhill Bridge - Burnhill Lane - Owler Lane - Badsworth.*

 - 1:25,000 Explorer Series No. 278 - Sheffield & Barnsley.

 & START - No official one but roadside parking beside church, on Main Street. Grid Ref: SE464149.

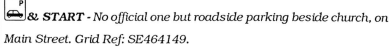 *- None on the walk - sorry!*

ABOUT THE WALK - Badsworth is a particularly attractive village and well worth wandering around. The walk takes you over the fields to Ackworth where you can link into the Ackworth walk to make a 9 mile circuit. The gently rolling countryside is a delight to walk in and although many of the fields are full of crops, the paths are well used and well defined. The section from Low Ackworth to Burnhill Bridge is particularly attractive beside a stream. Altogether a really enjoyable walk in the eastern corner of the county.

WALKING INSTRUCTIONS - Starting on Main Street beside the church, dedicated to St. Mary, walk up the road and follow it round sharply to your left. On the corner here is the entrance to Badsworth Hall. A few yards later turn right onto Ninevah Lane. In 1/4 mile pass Nineveh Farm on your left and a few yards later reach a solitary house on your right. Keep straight ahead on the hedged path and soon enter a cluster of trees and gain a stile. The path is defined and basically follows the field edge and not as marked on the Ordnance Survey map. The path curves left then right as you pass under electric power lines. Just after you keep straight ahead across the field and reach a track. Follow this slightly to your left and walk through the tunnel beneath the railway line. On the other side leave the track, which heads for Moor House, and turn right following the path which passes just to the right of a barn. Beyond you descend slightly to a footbridge and stile.

Over this aim for the lefthand corner of the field where there is a bridge. Cross this and keep straight ahead to a stile with Low Farm on your left. You now basically keep to the field hedge on your right and after the second field and stile you swing left to another stile and path sign at the road at Low Ackworth.

Turn right and in 1/4 mile pass Lee Lane on your left. (If you want to do the Ackworth circuit you should turn left up here.) A few yards later turn right onto Tan House Lane and follow this road which soon becomes a track as you regain the open countryside again. 1/4 mile past the last house pass a footbridge on your right -which don't use - and shortly after a small farm bridge with one side a metal rail. Don't cross this but instead follow the path close to the stream on your right as you walk along the field edge and pass under the six arched railway viaduct. You now keep to the field edge and beside the stream on your right for almost a mile to the track at Burnhill Bridge. Turn right, as bridlepath signed, and cross the "new" bridge with the old bridge beside it. The track - Burnhill Lane is wide and stone flagged to start with. Keep straight ahead on this track for 3/4 mile to the minor road from Thorpe Audlin. Turn right and opposite is Rogerthorpe Manor. In 60 yards leave the road on your right at the kissing gate and follow the defined path beside the field edge to another kissing gate and fenced path, which you follow to Badsworth church and Main Street where you began.

Row of Cottages, Badsworth.

Badsworth Hall.

Footbridge over River Went - Badsworth Walk.

HORBURY CUT - 6 MILES

N

River Calder

Locks

Broad Cut

Navigation Inn

Path to locks

Horbury Cut

HORBURY

A642 Wakefield

Ship Inn

The Bingley Arms

HORBURY BRIDGE

RIVER CALDER

CALDER & HEBBLE NAVIGATION

B6117 Netherton

A642 Huddersfield

Horse & Jockey Inn

HORBURY CUT
- 6 MILES
- allow 2 1/4 hours.

▀▄ ▄▀ ▀▀ ▄▀ *- Horbury Bridge - River Calder - Navigation Inn - Horbury Cut - Horbury Bridge.*

 - 1:25,000 Explorer Series No. 278 - Sheffield & Barnsley.

and start - No official one but roadside parking at Horbury Bridge - near Post Office. Grid Ref. SE282181.

- The Bingley Arms, Horse & Jockey and Ship Inn at Horbury Bridge. Navigation Inn beside Horbury Cut.

ABOUT THE WALK - a magnificent walk beside the River Calder before crossing a footbridge over the river beneath the railway bridge. Here you gain the Navigation Inn located on a triangle of land before walking beside the Horbury Cut of the Calder and Hebble Navigation. Throughout much of the walk the imposing tower and spire of Horbury church stands out clearly on the skyline. The cut is popular with narrowboats and you will no doubt see boats passing though the locks. The walk is done in a clockwise direction.

WALKING INSTRUCTIONS - Opposite the Ship Inn on the other-side of the A642 road is the path sign. Gain this and walk along the tarmaced drive keeping to the left of a motor repair works and next a car breakers yard. In a 100 yards gain the bank of the River Calder. The path is defined but in summer can be overgrown in places. Keep to the bank side with the river on your right for well over two miles. Little over a mile you pass under a railway bridge before following the river around a large loop with a sewerage works. The other side you walk beside the weirs and gain a tarmaced path just before your second railway bridge. Here turn right and ascend the steps and walk underneath the railway bridge across the river to a minor road. Keep straight ahead and pass the Navigation Inn on your right. There is a public right of way to your left which will take you to the locks at Broad Cut before the River Calder. There you can turn right and walk along the righthand side of the canal back to Horbury Bridge.

From the Navigation Inn continue ahead and cross the bridge over the canal before turning right. At first the path is not clear but aim for the railway bridge and close to the canal you find the path and tunnel through the bridge. Just after the path is clear as you reach a lock. Continue with the canal on your right to a stile. Just after ascend and descend round the remains of a coal tipper and just after you will have to ascend and descend again BEFORE the railway bridge to get round a wet area and quarry. The path is defined again and level walking to a stile on the edge of Hartley Bank Wood. Continue for more than 1/4 mile to the bridge over the canal. Cross over and for the remainder of the walk keep to the righthand bank of the canal and in 3/4 mile gain Horbury Bridge at The Bingley Arms. Turn right along the A642 road over the canal and river and regain The Ship Inn and Horbury Bridge.

CALDER & HEBBLE NAVIGATION - The navigation from Wakefield to Sowerby Bridge and the junction of the Rochdale Canal was completed in 1774. The Rochdale Canal was abandoned in 1952 but much of the navigation is still in use today. Horbury is worth exploring and Horbury church dedicated to St.Peter and St. Leonard is an exceptional building. Built in 1791 and designed by John Carr, who was born in Horbury and is buried beneath the church.

Ferrybridge walk - River Aire, Golden Lion Inn and junction of the Aire & Calder Navigation.

Aspley Basin, Huddersfield Narrow Canal.

Huddersfield Narrow Canal.

NEWMILLERDAM COUNTRY PARK - 2 1/2 MILES

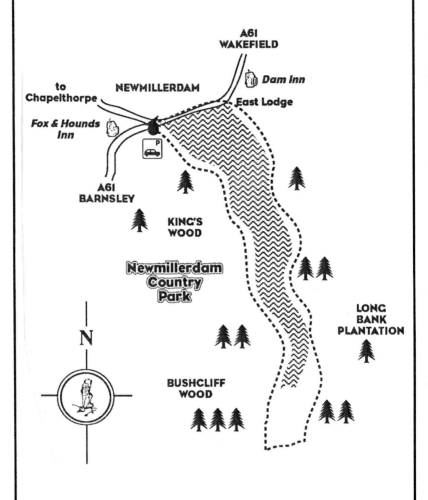

NEWMILLERDAM - as the name suggests the lake was originally made and used to feed a corn mill at its western end.

NEWMILLERDAM COUNTRY PARK
- 2 1/2 MILES
- allow 1 hour.

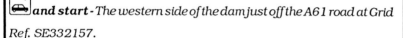 *- The encirlement of the dam in the woodland of Kings Wood and Bushcliff Wood.*

 - 1:25,000 Explorer Series No. 278 - Sheffield & Barnsley.

 and start *- The western side of the dam just off the A61 road at Grid Ref. SE332157.*

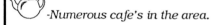 *- Fox & Hounds, Dam Inn at Newmillerdam.*

-Numerous cafe's in the area.

ABOUT THE WALK - A beautiful walk around the lake in an anti-clockwise direction, half in woodland and half close to the shore. The dam is full of waterfowl and a wide variety of birds will be seen. In June the rhoderdendrons are out adding to the attractive scene. The walk is designed to take you the length of the park but towards its southern end you have the option of crossing the lake in two places, shortening your walk.

WALKING INSTRUCTIONS - Walk to the lakeside from the carpark and turn right onto a wide track with the lake on your left. Keep on the track for more than 1/2 mile to a fork in the track. The one to your left takes you across the lake to the other side - you join up later. Continue ahead and soon cross a wide footbridge and a little later the track bears left to cross to the other side. Continue ahead by bearing slightly right then left and continue on a not so well used track as you walk through pine trees to the southern end of the wood. Here turn left and cross a bridge before following the track round to your left. At the next track junction, less than 1/4 mile later turn left and descend the track to the lakeside. You now keep close to the water's edge for more than 1/2 mile to the A61 road. Gaining the road turn left along it and left again back to the car park.

BRETTON COUNTRY PARK
- 3 1/2 MILES

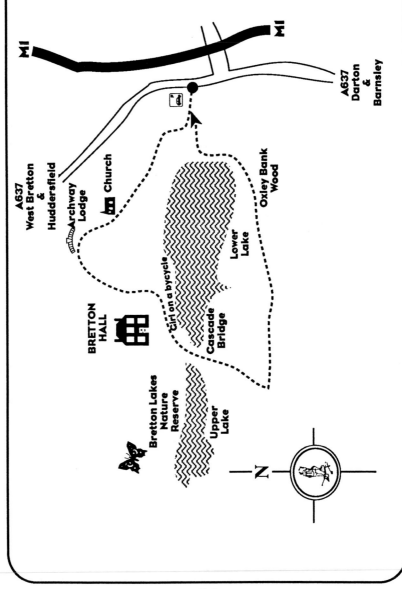

M1

M1

A637
Darton
&
Barnsley

Oxley Bank
Wood

Church

A637
West Bretton
&
Huddersfield

Archway
Lodge

Lower
Lake

Girl on a bycycle

Cascade
Bridge

BRETTON
HALL

Bretton Lakes
Nature
Reserve

Upper
Lake

N

BRETTON
COUNTRY PARK
- 3 1/2 MILES
- allow 1 1/2 hours.

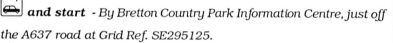 *- The encirclement of the Upper and Lower lakes, visiting key sites, the Yorkshire Sculpture Park and a fragment of the Cal-Der-Went Way. Walked in an anti-clockwise direction.*

 - 1:25,000 Explorer Series No. 278 - Sheffield & Barnsley.

 and start *- By Bretton Country Park Information Centre, just off the A637 road at Grid Ref. SE295125.*

- None on this walk - sorry!

ABOUT THE WALK - Bretton Country Park is a particularly attractive area with imposing house, extensive lakes and rich wood-land. The walk encircles the estate visiting the Bretton Church, Archway Lodge, the Yorkshire Sculpture Park on the the northern side. The southern half is through woodland and open countryside with impressive views of the surrounding area. The area is full of wild life with swans, coots, moorhens and Canada Geese on the lakes and grey squirrels galore in the woodland.

WALKING INSTRUCTIONS - Starting from the car park walk to the small gate well to the left of the Information Centre, and enter Bretton Country Park. In a few yards reach a track and bear right along it - you are following yellow arrows and topped posts for the first mile of the walk (to the entrance to the Sculpture Park). Keep on the track for the next 1/4 mile, noticing the red route turns left after a short distance; it is along this path you will be returning. Continue past a fenced clump of trees on your left and soon after reach a stile to the left of the gate. Turn right and cross the track and ascend past the entrance to Bretton church. Keep close to the field boundary - a wall - to the top righthand corner of the field with the impressive Gateway Lodge on your right.

Follow the field boundary round to your left - now a fence - and where the fence turns right keep straight ahead, guided by yellow topped posts, to the field boundary opposite. Bear left as you near it and begin descending with the boundary well to your right. Cross a track and descend to the bottom righthand corner of the field. Here you leave the yellow topped posts and follow red ones for the rest of the walk. Turn right through the kissing gate and enter the Yorkshire Sculpture Park. A short distance into the park with Bretton Hall on your right, gain a track and follow this round to your left passing a couple of sculptures including one to *"a girl on a bicycle"*.

At the end of the track in woodland reach a stile and gate. Go over this and turn left on a well defined track - you are now on the Cal-Der-Went Way. Keep on the track over a bridge over a bridge dividing the Upper and Lower Lakes and continue now ascending in woodland to a gate with impressive pillars. You are now in open fields as you continue ascending on the track with a race-horse training track on your right. Partway up the gentle slope and approximately 1/4 mile from the pillars reach a path signpost. Here turn left and descend the well defined path across the field to a stile and on to a track with the remnants of a pond on your right. Keep ahead on the track and in a few yards leave it to follow the path on your right and ascend gently to the crest of Oxley Bank. Go through the stile and turn left to the steps and follow the wide path down through the trees to steps and track close to the shore of Lower Lake. Turn right along the track passing a small quarry on your right and impressive well dated 1685. Follow the track round to your left walking close to the eastern edge of the lake to a gate. Cross the bridge over the River Dearne and enter the parkland area again. Follow the path to your half right and regain your earlier track before reaching the car park where you began.

BRETTON COUNTRY PARK - the hall is a magnificent 18th century Palladian building, set in extensive grounds, was landscaped for Sir Thomas Wentworth. The hall is now a College of Education. The grounds are home to the Yorkshire Sculpture Park, opened in 1977 - admission free - with works by many well known sculptors including Henry Moore and Barbara Hepworth.

Denby Dale Pie Hall - Upper Denby walk -
Pie dish in foreground.

HAW PARK - 4 MILES

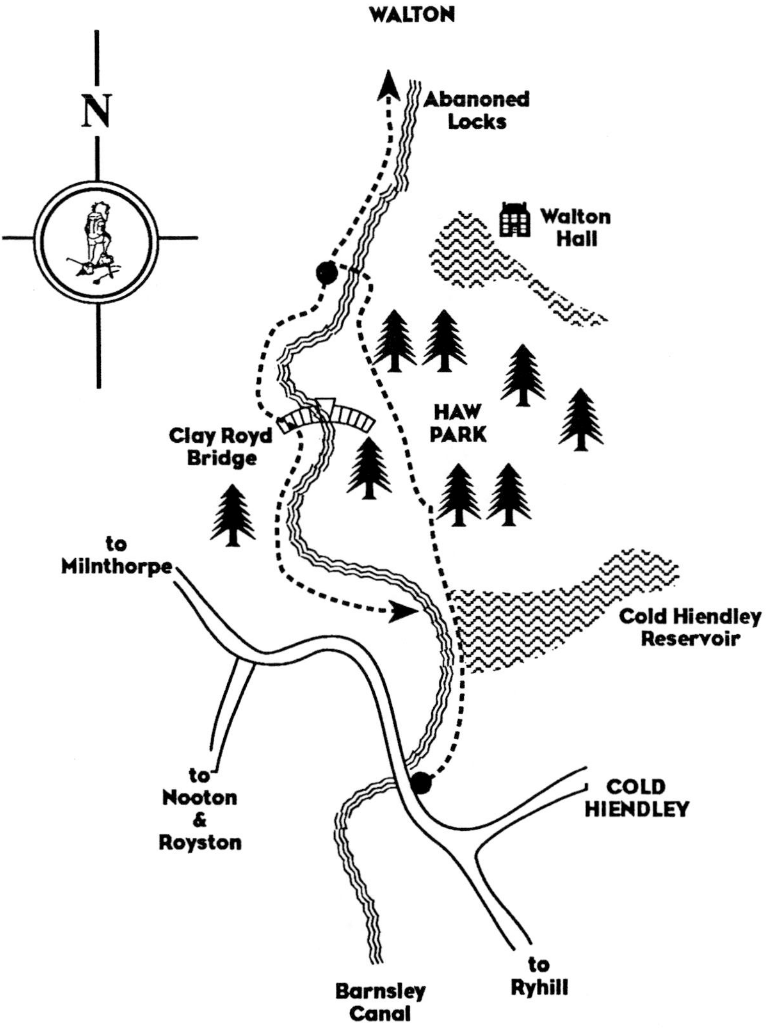

WALTON

N

Abanoned
Locks

Walton
Hall

HAW
PARK

Clay Royd
Bridge

to
Milnthorpe

Cold Hiendley
Reservoir

to
Nooton
&
Royston

COLD
HIENDLEY

to
Ryhill

Barnsley
Canal

HAW PARK
- 4 miles
- allow 1 1/2 hours.

- *Cold Hiendley Reservoir - Haw Park - Barnsley Canal - Overtown Bridge - Walton Hall Bridge - Walton Lock - Barnsley Canal - Cold Hiendley Reservoir.*

O.S. MAP - *1:25,000 Explorer Series No. 278 - Sheffield & Barnsley.*

P - *and Start - No official one but roadside parking at start of the walk at Grid Ref. SE 366143. Further parking along the track you walk beside Cold Hiendley Reservoir at Grid Ref. SE 367146.*

- *None on the walk. The nearest are at Notton and Wintersett.*

ABOUT THE WALK - Quite simply a magnificent walk - in fact one of the best canal walks I have done! First you walk past Cold Hiendley Reservoir before walking through Haw Park forest, which in autumn is particularly attractive. Leaving the wood behind you gain the abandoned Barnsley Canal and walk beside it to the remains of Walton Lock. Here you turn round and walk back along the canal to Cold Hiendley Reservoir. The scenery is most attractive and the canal beautifully engineered through a cutting and around the forest. En route are abandoned bridges and a feature I have never seen before in over 1,000 miles of canal walking - a guiding pulley for the horse rope around sharp corners of the canal. This walk just inside West Yorkshire is a walk of great historical importance and an absorbing exploration of canals.

WALKING INSTRUCTIONS - Starting from the road just before the canal, turn right onto the track with the canal on your left, as you walk to Cold Hiendley Reservoir. There is car parking space here. Continue along the lefthand edge of the reservoir and cross a footbridge to reach Haw Park forest. There are three paths here; take the middle one; the one on your left is the one you will return on. Walk

through the wood mostly on a track and keep straight ahead at all junctions in little over 1/2 mile you begin to descend and soon reach a stile close to a path sign - Cold Hiendley. Here you leave the forest behind and continue on a well defined path to the canal, which comes in from your left. Continue to a bridge over the canal and cross it. Just after turn right, as footpath signed and follow a path through the trees and down to the canal towpath. Don't turn right along the towpath; keep ahead instead on the towpath to Walton Hall bridge which has rope grooves. Cross the road and continue on the path to see the ruins of Walton Lock.

Here you turn round and retrace your steps back to Walton Hall bridge and to the towpath junction. Here you keep ahead on the towpath passing under the bridge you crossed earlier. You keep beside the canal on your left for the next mile as it passes through a cutting, and around Haw Park. En route passing bridges and two stone pulley posts. Near the end you walk along a filled in section before regaining the water filled canal. Shortly after pass under a bridge and regain your starting out path at the footbridge. Cross this and retrace your steps back to the road.

THE BARNSLEY CANAL - was opened in 1799 and joined Wakefield with Barnsley and the Dearne Canal. Sadly now abandoned but the section through Haw Park is outstanding with pulley blocks around which the tow rope was placed and the narrow boat "led" around the bend.

**ROPE PULLEY PILLAR
- BARNSLEY CANAL IN HAW PARK.**

BARNSLEY CANAL IN HAW PARK.

FARNLEY TYAS AND CASTLE HILL - 3 MILES

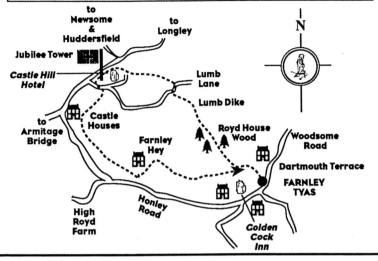

CASTLE HILL - The ramparts of an Iron Age fort can be seen but standing as a major landmark is the Jubilee Tower built in 1898-90 to celebrate the 60th anniversary of Queen Victoria's reign. Inside is an exhibition detailing the last 4,000 years of the history of the hill. In the 12th century the de Lacy family built a castle here but only the well remains.

(from opposite page)

Cross over to a stile and footpath sign and ascend the righthand side of the field to a stile and continue to another. Cross a track to your left to another stile and continue ascending beside the righthand edge of the field as it curves round to your left. Turn right and walk along the road to Castle Hill and Hotel. Now you can savour the view. Turn left along the edge past the tower and descend steps to the road. Turn left and in 100 yards turn right onto a path infront of the first building on your right. The path keeps to the lefthand edge of the fields to Castle Houses, little over 1/4 mile away. Gaining the houses turn left on another path which is well stiled. Cross seven fields, guided by stiles and in just over 1/2 mile gain the drive of Farnley Hey. Turn left along it and at the end of the buildings bear right at the stile and follow the well defined path to another stile. Keep the wall on your left to another stile where turn right along a walled track. This soon becomes a path and for the next 1/2 mile to your starting out path, you have a very well defined stiled path to follow. Gain the track you descended at the start and retrace your steps back to Farnley Tyas.

FARNLEY TYAS
AND
CASTLE HILL
- 3 MILES

- allow just over an hour.

- Farnley Tyas - Royd House Wood - Lumb Dike - Lumb Lane - Castle Hill - Castle Houses - Farnley Heys - Farnley Tyas.

 - 1:25,000 Explorer Series No. 288 - Bradford & Huddersfield.

 and start - *no official one at Farnley Tyas. Grid Ref. SE165128*

 - Golden Cock Inn, Farnley Tyas; Castle Hill Hotel, Castle Hill.

ABOUT THE WALK - A really short walk on good paths. There is a car park at Castle Hill but it would be wrong to start the walk from there, for you will see the best bit first! It is better to start from Farnley Tyas and earn the magnificent view from Castle Hill over Huddersfield and the Holme and Colne valleys. To get there and back you follow paths across fields and woodland.

WALKING INSTRUCTIONS - From the crossroads in Farnley Tyas, beside the Golden Cock Inn, take the lefthand road - Woodsome Road - for a few yards to Dartmouth Terrace. Just before it turn left down a track which is footpath signed. In 100 yards the track turns sharp left and in a few more yards leave it at a gate and turn sharp right down the field with the field boundary on your right. You return to the track on your way back. Descend to a stile and enter Royd Wood Wood. The path is defined through the wood to a stile. Cross a few yards of open country to another stile and re-enter woodland again. Continue on the path to another stile on the wood's edge. Descend to the lefthand field corner to a stile and descend through woodland to a footbridge over Lumb Dike. Ascend to stiles and steps and leave the woodland behind. At the corner of the field turn right and keep the field boundary on your left as you curve round to Lumb Lane.

(CONTINUED ON PAGE OPPOSITE)

MELTHAM AND MAG DALE - 6 1/2 MILES

MAG DALE

Mag Bridge

HONLEY

to Netherton

Spring Wood

Hill Top

Clitheroe Wood

Mag Brook

Cranby Farm

B6l08 Netherton

Honley Old Wood

Factory

Hall Dike

Honley Wood

to Honley

Far Fields

Meltham Mills

Greasy Slack Wood

Knowle Lane

Blackmoorfoot Reservoir

B6l08 MELTHAM

MELTHAM

N

MELTHAM AND MAG DALE
- 6 1/2 MILES
- allow 2 1/2 hours.

 - *Mag Bridge - Spring Wood - Hill Top - Bank Wood - Far Fields - Meltham Mills - Greasy Slack Wood - Honley Wood - Granby Farm - Mag Brook - Mag Bridge.*

 - 1:25,000 Explorer Series No. 288 - Bradford & Huddersfield.

 and start *- no official car park at Mag Dale. The walk starts at Mag Bridge - Grid Ref. SE136124 - which is on a narrow lane between Mag Dale and Honley; you may have to park a little way from the start.*

- None on the walk. Nearest at Honley or Meltham.

ABOUT THE WALK - A very pleasant walk around a scenic valley, through woodland and along lanes. The whole area bristles with right of ways and is worth exploring further.

WALKING INSTRUCTIONS - Starting from Mag Bridge close to Mag Brook, go through the kissing gate and follow a walled track for a few yards to a stile on your left. Cross this and nearby is Spring Head Well, keep on the path through Spring Wood and in a 1/3 mile where the path forks keep to the righthand path - the one on the left is the one you will be returning on. The path now begins to ascend, still in woodland to a gate. Through this you are now on a drive - Hilltop Bank - and ascend to the junction at Hill Top. Turn left and descend a walled path to a minor road. Cross over to another walled path beside house No. 41. Follow the path round to your left and cross a field to a footbridge. Cross the next to a gate and in the next field you soon have a hedge on your right as you reach some buildings and a drive which you follow to Hawthorn Cottage, minor road, and factory. Turn right and pass under a railway bridge and bear left to a road - B6108. Turn

right to stile and footpath sign. Ascend to Bank Wood and a stile. Continue through the wood to another stile and continue ascending a shallow "dale" guided by stiles to Far Fields Lane - a walled track - four fields from the wood.

Turn left along the track and in 150 yards where it turns right, go through the stile on your left and begin descending Far Fields, guided by stiles to a drive. Descend this and follow it round to your right to a building where turn left and descend to a footbridge. Follow the path round to a stile and cross a track and gain another footbridge before crossing an old railway line. Continue through a mill to the B6108 road. To your left is Fred Lawton's factory. Turn slightly right - not sharp right - and walk along Meltham Mills Road past the large mill complex on your left. Keep left at the next two junctions to gain Knowle Lane. Close to house No. 10 turn left, as footpath signed, and follow the well defined path/track into Greasy Slack Wood. In 1/4 mile take the lefthand path and a 1/3 mile later the lefthand one again as you enter Honley Wood. Keep just inside the wood to reach a track in another 1/3 mile; follow this to a lane and bear right along it. In 150 yards pass Granby Farm on your left. 1/4 mile later at a cross roads keep straight ahead. A further 1/4 mile pass a farm below you and turn left - as footpath signed - along a track past the farm to a bridge over Mag Brook. Cross the bridge and field to Spring Wood, where you were before. Turn right and follow your starting out path back to Mag Bridge.

Upper Denby walk - Cobbled path from Upper Denby to Denby Dale.

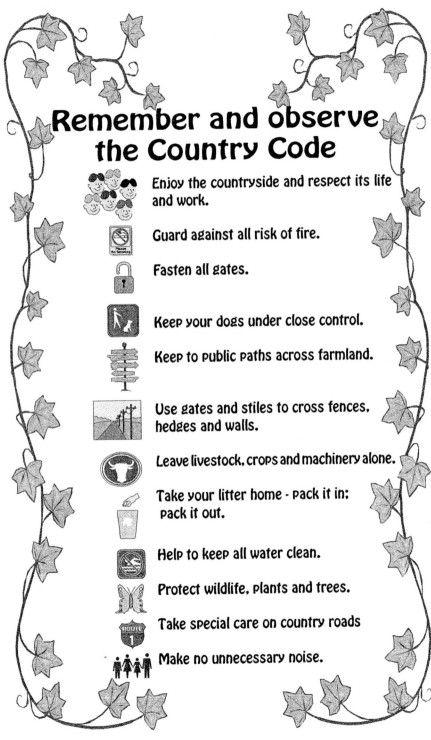

Remember and observe the Country Code

Enjoy the countryside and respect its life and work.

Guard against all risk of fire.

Fasten all gates.

Keep your dogs under close control.

Keep to public paths across farmland.

Use gates and stiles to cross fences, hedges and walls.

Leave livestock, crops and machinery alone.

Take your litter home - pack it in; pack it out.

Help to keep all water clean.

Protect wildlife, plants and trees.

Take special care on country roads

Make no unnecessary noise.

DENBY DALE
- BAGDEN PARK - 3 MILES

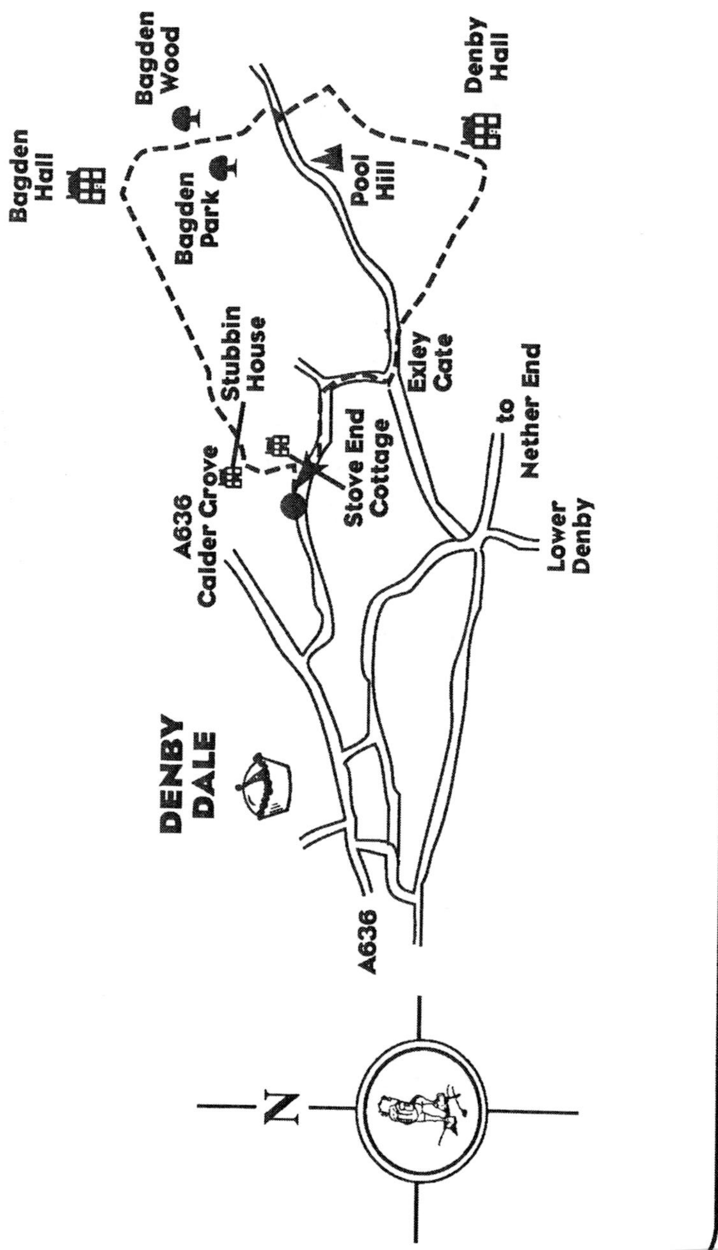

Bagden Wood

Denby Hall

Bagden Hall

Bagden Park

Pool Hill

Stubbin House

Exley Gate

A636 Calder Grove

Stove End Cottage

to Nether End

Lower Denby

DENBY DALE

A636

N

DENBY DALE
- BAGDEN PARK
- 3 MILES
- allow 1 hour.

 Denby Dale (East side) - Stubbin House - Bagden Park - Bagden Hall - Bagden Wood - Upper Bagden - Denby Hall - Exley Gate - Denby Dale (East Side).

O.S. MAP *- 1:25,000 Explorer Series No. 288 - Bradford & Huddersfield.*

and start - No official one but road side parking near start at Grid Ref. SE238087.

- none on the walk, nearest in Denby Dale itself.

ABOUT THE WALK - A short walk on the eastern side of Denby Dale around Bagden Park area. Very pleasant walking with several fine buildings on the way. The walk can be extended to include the walk that explores the western side of Denby Dale.

WALKING INSTRUCTIONS - From the start on the lane at Grid Ref. SE238087, descend, as footpath signed to Stove End Cottage and follow the track on the left of it. Where it divides turn right and walk past the righthand side of Stubbin House, guided by stiles. Continue across the fields to a small wood and stream. Cross a footbridge to a kissing gate and guided by kissing gates enter and cross Bagden Park. After the second kissing gate you follow a track to another kissing gate beside a lodge. Bear left along the hall drive to Bagden Hall and at the drive junction, 1/4 mile later close to the hall, turn right. In a few yards turn right at a kissing gate and steps and ascend to another kissing gate. Continue with the fence on your left to steps into Bagden Wood. Cross the wood to a stile and farmland. Continue straight ahead up the field before bearing left towards Upper Bagden and a minor road. Turn right then left onto a track which at first goes around Pool Hill before descending to Denby Hall. Beside the hall turn right at the stile and footpath sign and keep the fence on your right to a gate. Through this ascend a large open field to a stile to the left of a solitary tree. Continue with a wall on your left to a minor road. Turn left to the road junction at Exley Gate. Turn right and follow the road round to your left back to your starting point.

UPPER DENBY
AND GUNTHWAITE - 6 MILES

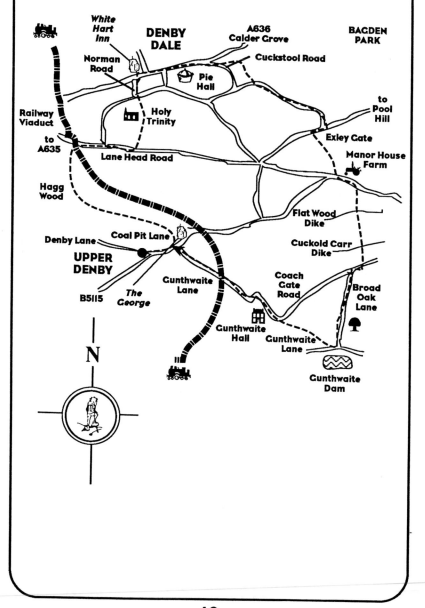

White Hart Inn

DENBY DALE

A636 Calder Grove

BAGDEN PARK

Norman Road

Cuckstool Road

Pie Hall

to Pool Hill

Railway Viaduct

Holy Trinity

Exley Gate

to A635

Manor House Farm

Lane Head Road

Hagg Wood

Flat Wood Dike

Denby Lane

Coal Pit Lane

Cuckold Carr Dike

UPPER DENBY

Coach Gate Road

Broad Oak Lane

Gunthwaite Lane

B5115

The George

Gunthwaite Hall

Gunthwaite Lane

N

Gunthwaite Dam

UPPER DENBY
AND
GUNTHWAITE
- 6 MILES
- allow 2 1/2 hours.

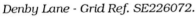 *- Upper Denby - Hagg Wood - Denby Dale - Pie Hall - Exley Gate - Nether End - Flat Wood Dike - Broad Wood - Broad Oak Lane - Gunthwaite Lane - Gunthwaite Hall - Upper Denby.*

 - 1:25,000 Explorer Series No. 288 - Bradford & Huddersfield.

 ***and start** - no official one but roadside parking at Upper Denby on Denby Lane - Grid Ref. SE226072.*

- The George, Upper Denby; White Hart Inn, Denby Dale.

ABOUT THE WALK - An outstanding walk through ever changing countryside. You follow old stone flagged paths, cross streams, walk through woodland, have extensive views, see ancient buildings and historical trees, and a pie dish from the famed Denby Dale Pie. The tradition goes back to 1788 when a massive pie was made to celebrate the recovery of George 111. There was an infamous pie riot in 1846 and in 1964 the pie was consumed by more than 30,000 people. Near Gunthwaite is an ancient oak tree and at Gunthwaite a historical barn. Part of the walk is in South Yorkshire.

The walk can be extended by following the Denby Dale/Bagden Park route, making a round walk of about 8 miles.

WALKING INSTRUCTIONS - Starting from Denby Lane in Upper Denby. Walk down the road to the T junction and turn left past the church, dedicated to St. John the Evangelist dating from 1627. A little further on your right is Gunthwaite Lane which is your return route. A few yards later and before The George inn turn left to the Post Office.

Cross the road to your right to Coal Pit Lane. A short distance along here turn left with a play area on your right. The track brings you to a small road beside some houses. Cross over to a stile and follow the path to a bridleway junction. Basically keep straight ahead onto a walled track - a bridleway. You soon start descending a magnificent stone flagged path which curves round to your left beside Hagg Wood. Eventually you reach the fringe of Denby Dale with a massive railway viaduct on your right. Turn right and 60 yards along the minor road - Lane Head Road - turn left at the stile and descend to Holy Trinity church, passing it on its righthand side, along Trinity Drive. At the road junction keep straight ahead and walk up Norman Road to the A636 road. Turn right past the main shopping area in Denby Dale, passing the White Hart Inn and library. Just after on your right is Pie Hall, and a pie dish now serving as a flower bed.

A few yards later with the cricket field below you turn right down Cuckstool Road. In the bottom near house No. 9 turn left then right and cross a footbridge over the River Dearne and ascend a walled track. Gaining the road at the top turn left along it and in just over 1/4 mile follow the road round to your right to the T junction at Exley Gate. Turn right and in a few yards left at the stone slab stile beside a small footpath sign. Cross the field to a stile and afterwards keep the field boundary on your right to reach another stile and minor road near Manor House Farm. Turn left to the farm and opposite it, as footpath signed, go through the gate. The pathline keeps to the high ground above a small dike on your left to gain a stone slabbed stile. Cross this and descend to a footbridge over Flat Wood Dike - you are now in South Yorkshire! Ascend to another stone stile and keep the wall on your left beyond over a rise and descend to another stile on the edge of Broad Wood. Follow the path down to your right to a stone slab over Cuckold Carr Dike and ascend to your left for a few yards to a stile. Over this keep straight ahead with the wall on your right to gain a stile beside a footpath sign.

Turn right along the lane and in a few yards turn left along Broad Oak Lane. After 1/4 mile pass Far Broad Oak and just after Near Broad Oak. To the right of the building can be seen the remains of the ancient oak tree - Broad Oak. Continue on the lane and descend to Gunthwaite Dam. Turn right, as bridlepath signed, and walk along Gunthwaite Lane which proves to be a magnificent flagged path. In less than 1/2 mile reach Gunthwaite Hall. Bear right but not sharp right, and follow the lane past the farm on your left, noticing the impressive historical barn on your left. Follow the lane - still Gunthwaite Lane - past woodland on your left and over a railway line before passing Gunthwaite Gate Lodge on your left. Continue on the lane into Upper Denby and back into West Yorkshire. Turn left and retrace your steps back past the church to Denby Lane where you started.

Broad Oak.

Barn, Gunthwaite.

HOLMFIRTH & RAMSDEN RESERVOIR - 7 MILES

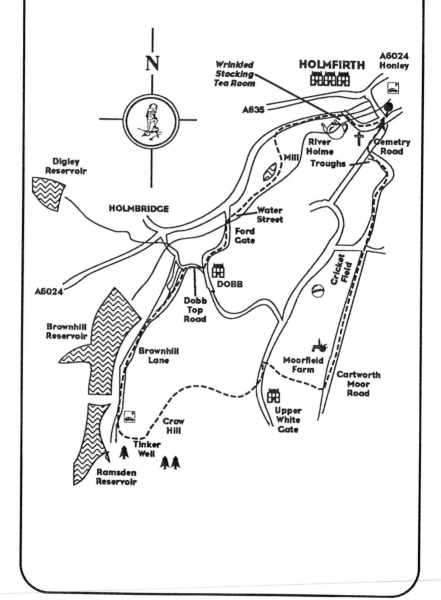

HOLMFIRTH & RAMSDEN RESERVOIR
- 7 MILES
- allow 2 1/2 hours.

👣 👣 *- Holmfirth - Bottoms - River Holme - Hinchcliffe Mill - Dobb - Brownhill Reservoir - Ramsden Reservoir - Crow Hill - Upper White Gate - Cartworth Moor Road - New Dunsley - Holmfirth.*

 - 1:25,000 Explorer Series No. 288 - Bradford & Huddersfield.

🅿️ **and start** *- Central Holmfirth.*

🍺 *- Numerous inns and cafe's in Holmfirth, including Sid's Cafe and the Wrinkled Stocking Tearoom. Victoria Inn, Prickleden 1/2 mile out on walk!*

ABOUT THE WALK - A walk in the *"last of the Summer Wine"* country. You see several places associated with the hit television show. The walk is a mixture of lane and moorland walking, firstly along a road out of Holmfirth before walking beside the River Holme. You gently ascend to Brownhill and Ramsden Reservoirs before climbing onto moorland with distant views. You return along quiet lanes, descending back to Holmfirth. A great walk on the edge of the Peak District National Park.

WALKING INSTRUCTIONS - Cross the road from the car park and bear right, not along the main street but along Hollowgate with the River Holme on your right. Follow the road round over a small bridge to the main road (A6024), with the Toll House Bookshop on your left. Turn left along the main road - Woodhead Road - and follow it for almost 3/4 mile. Almost immediately on your left is the *"Wrinkled Stocking Tearoom"*. Follow the road past the Victoria Inn on your right and more than 1/4 mile later near house No. 81, turn left as footpath signed and descend to the mill pond of Bottoms Mill. Follow the path

round to your right with the mill pond on your right and the River Holme on your left. In less than 1/2 mile enter Water Street. Just after at road junction turn left along Ford Gate and ascend towards the village of Dobb. Entering the village take the first road - Dobb Top Road - on your right and follow it round past the houses on your left and where the road forks keep to the lefthand one. 1/4 mile later the road at a small road junction bear left along Broomhill Lane and very soon on your right is Broomhill Reservoir. Walk along the lane above the reservoir to the beginnings of Ramsden Reservoir with a car park on your left.

At the car park turn left, as footpath signed and follow a track and ascend beside woodland on your right. In less than 1/4 mile close to Tinker Well at a crossroads of footpaths, turn left to a ladder stile and foot-bridge, and follow the path beside a wall on your left. The path curves round to your right beneath Crow Hill and soon becomes a walled track. Follow it round, passing through gates and keep to the lefthand track to gain the top of Dobb Dike. Just after the track curves round to your right to a road, gained by a gate beside a footpath sign. To your right is Upper White Gate. Turn left then right along a walled track. In 1/4 mile at the first crossroads, turn left along another walled track - Cartworth Moor Road. This becomes a tarmaced surface at Moorfield Farm. 1/2 mile later pass a cricket field on your left and gain a cross roads.

Go straight across and keep on a walled track which curves round to your right and in 1/2 mile at New Dunsley turn left and in 100 yards left again and descend to a road with water troughs on your left. Turn right along - Cemetery Road - passing the cemetery on your left in 1/4 mile. Continue descending towards Holmfirth and at the road junction bear left along Rotcher Road and descend to Hollowgate where you began.

RAMSDEN RESERVOIR - Part of three reservoirs of which Brownhill is the biggest, supplying water to the Holme Valley. Together they have a holding capacity of 5.6 million gallons.

HOLMFIRTH - is now immortalised by the BBC T.V. series - "Last of the Summer Wine". Places associated with those lovable rogues Compo, Clegg and Seymour and Nora Batty can be seen. The town is worth exploring to see the ginnels - steep narrow cobbled paths - and other historical buildings, artists and the Postcard Museum.

The Wrinkled Stocking Tea Room, Holmfirth.

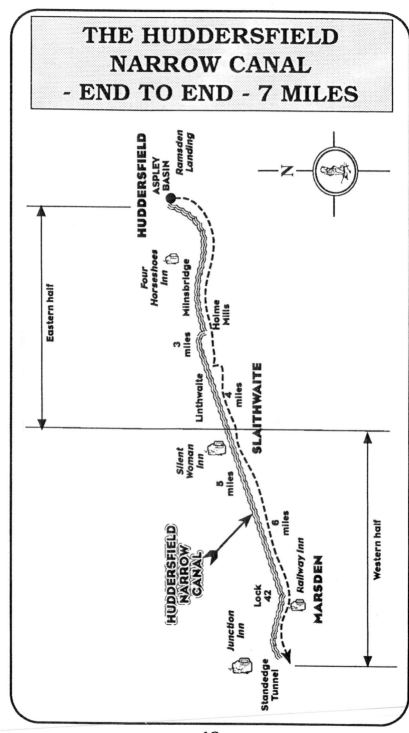

THE HUDDERSFIELD NARROW CANAL
- END TO END - 7 MILES

HUDDERSFIELD
ASPLEY BASIN
Ramsden Landing

Eastern half

Four Horseshoes Inn
Milnsbridge

3 miles

Holme Mills

Linthwaite

4 miles

SLAITHWAITE

Silent Woman Inn

5 miles

HUDDERSFIELD NARROW CANAL

6 miles

Railway Inn

Western half

Lock 42

MARSDEN

Junction Inn

Standedge Tunnel

N

THE HUDDERSFIELD NARROW CANAL END TO END - 7 1/2 MILES

- allow 3 hours.

- Huddersfield Central - Aspley Basin - Milnsbridge - Linthwaite - Slaithwaite - Marsden - Standedge Tunnel.

O.S. MAP *- 1:25,000 Explorer Series No. 288 - Bradford & Huddersfield.*

and start *- Marsden or Tunnel End.*

- Numerous in Huddersfield central area. In walking order from Aspley Basin - Packet Inn, Old Mother Riley's Inn, Four Horseshoes Inn; Commercial Inn, Silent Woman, Shoulder of Mutton Inn, Slaithwaite; Railway Inn, Marsden; Junction Inn near Tunnel End.

ABOUT THE WALK - Quite simply a truly outstanding canal walk from the industrial centre of Huddersfield to moorland at Marsden. The canal is full of history and for much of its length you can follow along the towpath. The permutations are numerous and you can do several circular walks rather than an end to end one, using Slaithwaite as the terminus. For the purposes of this book I have worked the route out leaving the car at Marsden Railway Station or at Tunnel End. If you do the latter you will have to walk along the canal to the Railway Station. Here you can either get a bus to central Huddersfield - they are frequent - or catch a train to Huddersfield. You can, of course, walk from Marsden to Huddersfield and back!

To get to Aspley Basin, the junction of the Broad and Narrow Huddersfield Canal, from the Railway Station turn right along Railway Street to Westgate and turn left and then right into Market Street. Turn left down King Street to its end at a major roundabout. Cross over to

the A629 Sheffield road and a few yards down here on your right is the access to the canal - the basin is on your left. From the Bus Station walk down Dundas Street to Market Street and turn left then right down King Street.

WALKING INSTRUCTIONS - Follow the towpath on the left of the canal for nearly 1/2 mile to the road at Fairfield Mill, en route passing Stanley Dawson Lock. The next 1/2 mile of canal cannot be walked beside. Turn left then right to the A616 road. Here turn right passing the Packet Inn and turn left soon afterwards along the A62 road. On your left is Setters Engineers and canal. Pass Old Mother Riley's Inn on your right and at the road junction just after turn left and in a few yards you can regain the canal close to Charlie Browns tyre and battery depot. Keep to the lefthand side of the canal. You soon cross an aqueduct and pass largely through industrial complexes for the next mile to the Four Horseshoes Inn. near Milnsbridge.

Continue beside the canal passing Stanley Mills on your right and over another aqueduct. You have now left the Huddersfield area and moving into rural countryside, becoming more attractive at every stride. Soon pass Holme Mills on your left and a 3 mile marker. Next pass Scarwood Bridge and the outskirts of Linthwaite and a 4 mile marker - from Aspley Basin. As you approach Slaithwaite the canal is filled in and just after Spa Works you follow a footpath only into Slaithwaite. Pass the Commercial Inn and Shoulder of Mutton Inn. Opposite you regain the line of the canal and up the road to your right is the Silent Woman Inn. Pass the Old Bank bridge and 5 mile marker and Upper Mills on your left. The canal is now totally rural passing through delightful countryside with moorland views ahead. Pass the 6 mile marker near Lingards Wood and in another mile you are back at Marsden. The Standedge Tunnel is 1/2 mile away and if you haven't seen the tunnel end of the canal it is worth walking there to see it and the Canal Information office.

ASPLEY BASIN - Junction of the Huddersfield Broad (Ramsden Canal) and Narrow canals, was completed in 1780. The Huddersfield Canal Society hold a festival here annually. Aspley Warehouse is believed to be the oldest surviving canal warehouse in Northern England being built in 1778. Here wool was stored after being brought up the Ramsden canal.

HUDDERSFIELD NARROW CANAL

HUDDERSFIELD NARROW CANAL - The canal was authorised by Act of Parliament in 1794 and completed seventeen years later in 1811. The canal joined the Calder Navigation with the Ashton Canal, which in turn linked with the Peak Forest Canal and Macclesfield Canal - part of the Cheshire Ring. The canal's greatest feature is the 3 miles 135 yards (4950 metres) long Standedge Tunnel; a huge undertaking and even by today's standard a magnificent engineering feat. The was no towpath and the horses were led over the hill via "Boat Lane". The narrow boats were legged through. The tunnel is often referred to as "one of the seven wonders of the waterways." The former tunnel keeper's cottage at the Marsden end is now a Canal and Countryside Centre and well worth visiting. By early this century the canal was little used and in 1944 was officially abandoned. Today it is one of the finest canal which is slowly being restored by the endeavours of the Huddersfield Canal Society.

Canal milepost.

Lock on Huddersfield Narrow Canal.

MARSDEN MOORS
- 9 MILES

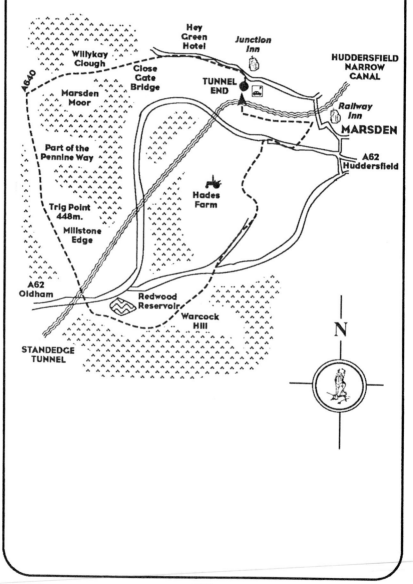

MARSDEN MOORS
- 9 MILES
- allow 3 1/2 hours

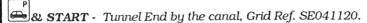 - *Tunnel End Car Park - Waters Lane - Hey Green - Willykay Clough - A640 - Pennine Way - Standedge - Millstone Edge - A62 - Warcock - Mount Road - Hades Farm - Marsden - Huddersfield Narrow Canal - Tunnel End.*

 - *1:25,000 Outdoor Leisure Map - No. 1 - The Dark Peak and No 21 - South Pennines.*

 & START - *Tunnel End by the canal, Grid Ref. SE041120.*

- Car park en route on A62 where Pennine Way crosses beside Brun Clough Reservoir - Grid Ref. SE018095.

- Junction Inn, Tunnel End. Railway Inn, Marsden by Lock No 42.

ABOUT THE WALK - a really superb moorland walk, starting from the northern end of the Standedge Tunnel of the Huddersfield Narrow Canal - other walks in the book explore the canal more fully. Although this walk is the longest in the book and not really a "short walk", it is nethertheless a walk of great character. You ascend Marsden Moors via Willykay Clough to join the Pennine Way at the A640 road. Here you follow the "way" over Millstone Edge and Standedge to the A62 road. Beneath you is the Standedge Tunnel. Here you leave the "way" and cross more moorland close to Redbrook Reservoir before descending to Marsden. The final 1/2 mile is along the canal back to Tunnel End. Marsden is the start or end of the challenging 25 mile Marsden to Edale walk.

WALKING INSTRUCTIONS - Walk back up the road from Tunnel End car park to the Junction Inn and turn left along Waters Road. Follow this no through road to just past the entrance to Hey Green Hotel; 3/4 mile away. Just past here and as you ascend the narrow lane, turn left, as signposted - Willykay Clough - and descend the footpath and follow it round by the brook to Close Gate Bridge, a splendid packhorse bridge. Turn right and in about 50 yards left and ascend the rock slabs via the zig-zag path. You are soon on the moors

and continue on the defined path and in 1/4 mile cross a small stream from Willykay Clough. Continue on the path gently ascending with the stream on your left. The path heads westwards and is well defined and has occasional solitary pillars with the words - "PH Road". You keep on this path for 1 1/2 miles from crossing the stream to the A640 road.

Don't cross the road, turn left, and follow the well defined and artificial path - The Pennine Way - for more than 1/2 mile over the moorland to start of Millstone Edge. Here as signposted turn left to walk along the gritstone edge and in 3/4 mile reach the trig point at 448 metres. Continue on the path to stiles and stone walls, with footpath signs of an owl and you join the "Oldham Way" as well as being on the "Pennine Way." In 1/4 mile reach a track and turn left along it to gain the A62 road and car park beside Brun Clough Reservoir.

Cross the road into the car park and turn left on the - still the Pennine Way - keeping close to the road on your left. Where the path leaves the road, the Pennine Way turns right to cross Rocher Moss. You keep ahead following a well defined track with Redbrook Reservoir on your left. Follow this track round and across Warcock Hill and descend to Mount Road. Cross it to Old Mount Road and leave it immediately, as footpath signed, and follow the track to Hades Farm, 3/4 mile away. Where the track turns sharp left to the farm beside another building on your right, turn right through the stile, as path signed, and descend past New Hey Farm. Beyond it the path bears right and at the field edge turn left to another stile and path sign. Here turn right and continue descending past the houses to the A62 road on the outskirts of Marsden. Turn right along the road and in 1/4 mile reach the church. Turn left down the path by its cemetery wall to a road. Turn right then left over a magnificent little bridge and turn right along the road - The Green. At the end turn left up Station Road passing the Railway Inn on your left. Just after gain the Huddersfield Narrow Canal at Lock 42. Turn left along the towpath and reach Tunnel End 1/2 mile later.

Close Gate Bridge.

THE HIKER'S CODE

❀ Hike only along marked routes - do not leave the trail.

❀ Use stiles to climb fences; close gates.

❀ Camp only in designated campsites.

❀ Carry a light-weight stove.

❀ Leave the trail cleaner than you found it.

❀ Leave flowers and plants for others to enjoy.

❀ Keep dogs on a leash.

❀ Protect and do not disturb wildlife.

❀ Use the trail at your own risk.

❀ Leave only your thanks and footprints
   - take nothing but photographs.

THE CALDERDALE WAY
- 51 MILES

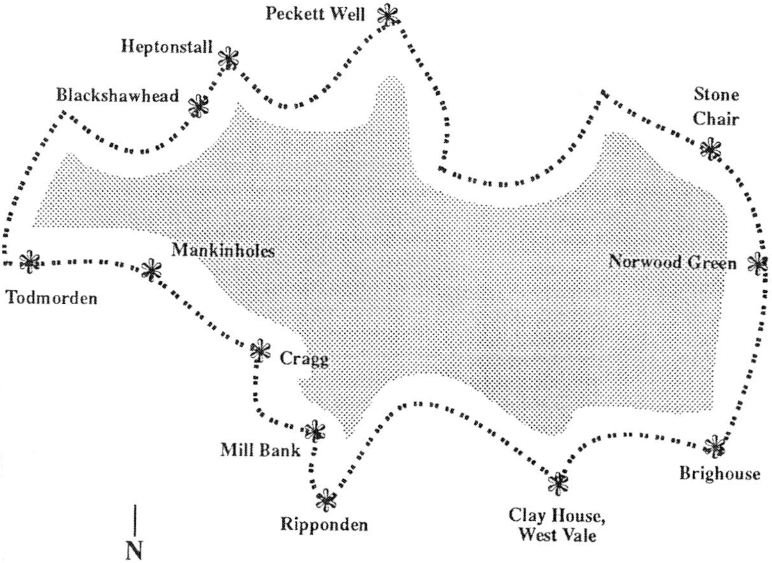

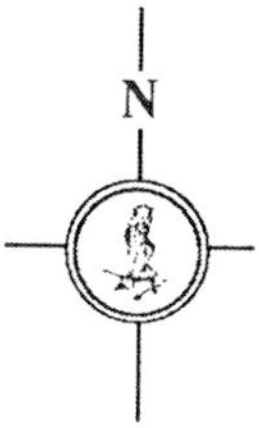

Peckett Well

Heptonstall

Blackshawhead

Stone Chair

Mankinholes

Norwood Green

Todmorden

Cragg

Mill Bank

Brighouse

Ripponden

Clay House, West Vale

N

THE CALDERDALE WAY - 51 MILES

I have done hundreds of "long walks" over the years and ever since giving a lecture in Halifax in 1979, I learnt of the Calderdale Way. The guide gathered dust on my "walks to do" shelf and it wasn't until 1995 that I did it! Even then it was literally on the spur of the moment. A copy of "Untrodden Ways" landed on my desk and looking through it saw a chapter on the Calderdale Way. I read it late on the Thursday night and on the Friday drove to the start and over the next two days walked it in blistering heat and saw no other walker!

Personally, I thought the Way was a magnificent circular route around the Pennines over remote moorlands, through attractive villages and hamlets, down into wooded valleys rich in history and distant views across the countryside that the Pennine Way crosses. I include this walk in this book to encourage you to embark along a longer route - whether you do it in stages over several weeks or simply walk it over a weekend as I did - I am sure you will have an enjoyable and interesting walk. I started on the Hebble & Calder Canal near Clay House and walked 25 miles to Blackshawhead and stayed overnight at the Shoulder of Mutton Inn - approximately half-way. The next day I completed the circuit of 26 miles back to Clay House. There are only two major amenity locations on the walk - Ripponden and Heptonstall. The latter is half-way and being near the Pennine Way has camping facilities nearby. There is a campsite at Jerusalem Farm near Saltonstall and a Youth Hostel at Mankinholes.

The first stage from Clay House, West Vale, near Elland, takes you onto moorland, an impressive edge and views across the valley to Halifax. You descend to Ripponden and the oldest inn in Yorkshire. You ascend back to the high country before descending to Cragg Vale with church dedicated to St. John in the Wilderness and the Hinchliffe Arms. Ascending once more you walk around Withens Reservoir and pass the Te Deum Stone, marking the summit of the packhorse route between Cragg and Mankinholes. Coffins were rested here on their journey to the cemetery. Soon after you get the view to Stoodley Pike - which is a landmark which you will see constantly for the next 15 miles - and cross the Pennine Way before descending to Mankinholes (the only YHA on the Way). You ascend again before descending to the fringe of Todmorden. Across the valley can be seen Dobroyd Castle, which you walk past. Afterwards you regain the high country and moorland before approaching Blackshawhead, the junction of several packhorse routes.

From Blackshawhead you cross fields before descending to a clapper bridge - Hebble Hole Bridge - and join the Pennine Way again. After a few yards you leave it and begin an impressive walk along gritstone edges to the outstandingly attractive village of Heptonstall above Hebden Bridge - half way point. You descend to Hebden Dale before ascending to Pecket Well. From here you walk along the edge of moorland for three miles before descending to Jerusalem Farm. You ascend steeply and climb steadily to Hunter Hill, which at 1,250ft is one of the highest points along the way. From Heptonstall until the end you will pass several inns. You descend gradually to Holdsworth before walking through the delightful Shibden Valley and crossing the fields to Stone Chair - the stone chair still remains and dates back to the coaching days. Your next goal is Norwood Green with many areas of open common land. You are now in the home straight as you descend to Brighouse and the Hebble and Calder Canal. You follow this a short distance before ascending above Southowram with extensive views. You descend past Exley Hall back to the canal and onto Clay House.

The whole routes is very well signposted - "Calderdale Way" and with a yellow logo - cw. The West Yorkshire CC and the Calderdale Way Association have produced a guide to the route.......Happy walking!

Descending to Mill Bank.

The attractive village of Heptonstall.

View to Cragg, Withens Reservoir and Stoodley Pike.

WALK RECORD CHART

Date walked

PONTEFRACT AREA -

FERRYBRIDGE - 3 MILES ....

ACKWORTH - 4 1/2 MILES ....

BADSWORTH - 5 MILES ....

WAKEFIELD AREA -

HORBURY CUT - 6 MILES ....

NEWMILLERDAM COUNTRY PARK - 2 1/2 MILES ....

BRETTON COUNTRY PARK - 3 1/2 MILES ....

HAW PARK - 4 MILES ....

HUDDERSFIELD AREA -

FARNLEY TYAS & CASTLE HILL - 3 MILES ....

MELTHAM & MAG DALE - 6 1/2 MILES ....

DENBY DALE & BAGDEN PARK - 3 MILES ....

UPPER DENBY & GUNTHWAITE - 6 MILES ....

HOLMFIRTH & RAMSDEN RESERVOIR - 7 MILES ....

HUDDERSFIELD NARROW CANAL - 3 WALKS

- End to End - 7 1/2 MILES ....

- Eastern circular - 7 1/2 MILES ....

- Western circular - 7 1/2 MILES ....

MARSDEN MOORS - 9 MILES ....

THE CALDERDALE WAY - 51 MILES ....

THE JOHN MERRILL WALK BADGE

Complete six walks in this book and get the above special embroidered badge and signed certificate. Badges are black cloth with lettering and man embroidered in four colours.

BADGE ORDER FORM

Date walks completed..

NAME ....

ADDRESS ....

....

Price: £4.00 each including postage, VAT and signed completion certificate. Amount enclosed (Payable to Walk & Write Ltd) ..
From: Walk & Write Ltd.,
Marathon House, Longcliffe,
Nr. Matlock, Derbyshire. DE4 4HN
Tel /Fax 01629 - 540991
********** YOU MAY PHOTOCOPY THIS FORM **********

"HAPPY WALKING!" T SHIRT
- Yellow (Sunflower) with black lettering and walking man logo.
Send £7.95 to Walk & Write Ltd., stating size required.
John Merrill's "Happy Walking!" Cap - £3.50
Happy Walking Button Badge - 50p inc p & p.

OTHER JOHN MERRILL WALK BOOKS

CIRCULAR WALK GUIDES -
SHORT CIRCULAR WALKS IN THE PEAK DISTRICT - Vol. 1,2 and 3
CIRCULAR WALKS IN WESTERN PEAKLAND
SHORT CIRCULAR WALKS IN THE STAFFORDSHIRE MOORLANDS
SHORT CIRCULAR WALKS - TOWNS & VILLAGES OF THE PEAK DISTRICT
SHORT CIRCULAR WALKS AROUND MATLOCK
SHORT CIRCULAR WALKS IN "PEAK PRACTICE COUNTRY."
SHORT CIRCULAR WALKS IN THE DUKERIES
SHORT CIRCULAR WALKS IN SOUTH YORKSHIRE
SHORT CIRCULAR WALKS IN SOUTH DERBYSHIRE
SHORT CIRCULAR WALKS AROUND BUXTON
SHORT CIRCULAR WALKS AROUND WIRKSWORTH
SHORT CIRCULAR WALKS IN THE HOPE VALLEY
40 SHORT CIRCULAR WALKS IN THE PEAK DISTRICT
CIRCULAR WALKS ON KINDER & BLEAKLOW
SHORT CIRCULAR WALKS IN SOUTH NOTTINGHAMSHIRE
SHORT CIRCULAR WALKS IN CHESHIRE
SHORT CIRCULAR WALKS IN WEST YORKSHIRE
WHITE PEAK DISTRICT AIRCRAFT WRECKS
CIRCULAR WALKS IN THE DERBYSHIRE DALES
SHORT CIRCULAR WALKS FROM BAKEWELL
SHORT CIRCULAR WALKS IN LATHKILL DALE
CIRCULAR WALKS IN THE WHITE PEAK
SHORT CIRCULAR WALKS IN EAST DEVON
SHORT CIRCULAR WALKS AROUND HARROGATE
SHORT CIRCULAR WALKS IN CHARNWOOD FOREST
SHORT CIRCULAR WALKS AROUND CHESTERFIELD
SHORT CIRCULAR WALKS IN THE YORKS DALES - Vol 1 - Southern area.
SHORT CIRCULAR WALKS IN THE AMBER VALLEY (Derbyshire)
SHORT CIRCULAR WALKS IN THE LAKE DISTRICT
SHORT CIRCULAR WALKS IN THE NORTH YORKSHIRE MOORS
SHORT CIRCULAR WALKS IN EAST STAFFORDSHIRE
DRIVING TO WALK - 16 Short Circular walks south of London by Dr. Simon Archer Vol 1 and 2
LONG CIRCULAR WALKS IN THE PEAK DISTRICT - Vol.1,2 ,3 and 4.
DARK PEAK AIRCRAFT WRECK WALKS
LONG CIRCULAR WALKS IN THE STAFFORDSHIRE MOORLANDS
LONG CIRCULAR WALKS IN CHESHIRE
WALKING THE TISSINGTON TRAIL
WALKING THE HIGH PEAK TRAIL
WALKING THE MONSAL TRAIL & OTHER DERBYSHIRE TRAILS
PEAK DISTRICT WALKING - TEN "TEN MILER'S" - Vol One and Two
CLIMB THE PEAKS OF THE PEAK DISTRICT
PEAK DISTRICT WALK A MONTH Vols One,Two, Three, and Four
TRAIN TO WALK Vol. One - The Hope Valley Line
DERBYSHIRE LOST VILLAGE WALKS -Vol One and Two.
CIRCULAR WALKS IN DOVEDALE AND THE MANIFOLD VALLEY
CIRCULAR WALKS AROUND GLOSSOP
WALKING THE LONGDENDALE TRAIL
WALKING THE UPPER DON TRAIL
THE HAPPY HIKER - WHITE PEAK - CHALLENGE WALK

CANAL WALKS -
VOL 1 - DERBYSHIRE & NOTTINGHAMSHIRE
VOL 2 - CHESHIRE & STAFFORDSHIRE
VOL 3 - STAFFORDSHIRE
VOL 4 - THE CHESHIRE RING
VOL 5 - LINCOLNSHIRE & NOTTINGHAMSHIRE
VOL 6 - SOUTH YORKSHIRE
VOL 7 - THE TRENT & MERSEY CANAL
VOL 8 - WALKING THE DERBY CANAL RING
VOL 9 - WALKING THE LLANGOLLEN CANAL

JOHN MERRILL DAY CHALLENGE WALKS -
WHITE PEAK CHALLENGE WALK
DARK PEAK CHALLENGE WALK
PEAK DISTRICT END TO END WALKS
STAFFORDSHIRE MOORLANDS CHALLENGE WALK
THE LITTLE JOHN CHALLENGE WALK
YORKSHIRE DALES CHALLENGE WALK

> **For a complete list of my titles please write to me at Walk & Write Ltd., or phone - 01629 - 540991**

NORTH YORKSHIRE MOORS CHALLENGE WALK
LAKELAND CHALLENGE WALK
THE RUTLAND WATER CHALLENGE WALK
MALVERN HILLS CHALLENGE WALK
THE SALTER'S WAY
THE SNOWDON CHALLENGE
CHARNWOOD FOREST CHALLENGE WALK
THREE COUNTIES CHALLENGE WALK (Peak District).
CAL-DER-WENT WALK by Geoffrey Carr,
THE QUANTOCK WAY
BELVOIR WITCHES CHALLENGE WALK
THE CARNEDDAU CHALLENGE WALK
THE SWEET PEA CHALLENGE WALK
THE LINCOLNSHIRE WOLDS - BLACK DEATH - CHALLENGE WALK

INSTRUCTION & RECORD -
HIKE TO BE FIT.....STROLLING WITH JOHN
THE JOHN MERRILL WALK RECORD BOOK
HIKE THE WORLD

MULTIPLE DAY WALKS -
THE RIVERS'S WAY
PEAK DISTRICT: HIGH LEVEL ROUTE
PEAK DISTRICT MARATHONS
THE LIMEY WAY
THE PEAKLAND WAY
COMPO'S WAY by Alan Hiley
THE BRIGHTON WAY by Norman Willis
THE WALSINGHAM WAY

COAST WALKS & NATIONAL TRAILS -
ISLE OF WIGHT COAST PATH
PEMBROKESHIRE COAST PATH
THE CLEVELAND WAY
WALKING ANGELSEY'S COASTLINE.
WALKING THE COASTLINE OF THE CHANNEL ISLANDS
THE WALSINGHAM WAY

DERBYSHIRE & PEAK DISTRICT HISTORICAL GUIDES -
A to Z GUIDE OF THE PEAK DISTRICT
DERBYSHIRE INNS - an A to Z guide
HALLS AND CASTLES OF THE PEAK DISTRICT & DERBYSHIRE
TOURING THE PEAK DISTRICT & DERBYSHIRE BY CAR
DERBYSHIRE FOLKLORE
PUNISHMENT IN DERBYSHIRE
CUSTOMS OF THE PEAK DISTRICT & DERBYSHIRE
WINSTER - a souvenir guide
ARKWRIGHT OF CROMFORD
LEGENDS OF DERBYSHIRE
DERBYSHIRE FACTS & RECORDS
TALES FROM THE MINES by Geoffrey Carr
PEAK DISTRICT PLACE NAMES by Martin Spray
DERBYSHIRE THROUGH THE AGES - DERBYSHIRE IN PREHISTORIC TIMES
SIR JOSEPH PAXTON
FLORENCE NIGHTINGALE
JOHN SMEDLEY
BONNIE PRINCE CHARLIE

JOHN MERRILL'S MAJOR WALKS -
TURN RIGHT AT LAND'S END
WITH MUSTARD ON MY BACK
TURN RIGHT AT DEATH VALLEY
EMERALD COAST WALK
JOHN MERRILL'S 1999 WALKER'S DIARY
A WALK IN OHIO
TURN LEFT AT GRANJA DE LA MORERUELA

SKETCH BOOKS -
SKETCHES OF THE PEAK DISTRICT

COLOUR BOOK:-
THE PEAK DISTRICT.......something to remember her by.

OVERSEAS GUIDES -
HIKING IN NEW MEXICO - Vol I - The Sandia and Manzano Mountains.
Vol 2 - Hiking "Billy the Kid" Country. Vol 4 - N.W. area - " Hiking Indian Country."
"WALKING IN DRACULA COUNTRY" - Romania.

VISITOR GUIDES - MATLOCK . BAKEWELL. ASHBOURNE.

Walk & Write Ltd

Marathon House,
Longcliffe, Nr. Matlock, Derbyshire. DE4 2HN
Tel/Fax 01629 -540991

YORKSHIRE BOOKS

ORDER FORM

	QTY
113 SHORT CIRCULAR WALKS IN *SOUTH YORKSHIRE - £5.95*	
207 LONG CIRCULAR WALKS IN SOUTH YORKSHIRE - £4.95	
305 SOUTH YORKSHIRE CANAL WALKS- £5.95	
965 CYCLING AROUND SHEFFIELD - £3.95	
146 WALKING THE UPPER DON TRAIL . £4.50 ....NEW	
115 SHORT CIRCULAR WALKS IN *WEST YORKSHIRE - £4.95*	
996 LAST OF THE DAY HOLE MINERS- £4.95...........NEW	
706 TALES FROM THE MINES - £3.95	
715 FURTHER TALES FROM THE MINES- £4.95	
508 COMPO'S WAY- £4.50 ....NEW	
506 THE CAL-DER-WENT WAY - ~£3.95	
971 PENNINE PENANCE - £3.95	
116 SHORT CIRCULAR WALKS IN THE *YORKSHIRE DALES - $4.95*	
406 YORKSHIRE DALES CHALLENGE WALK - £3.95	
122 SHORT CIRCULAR WALKS AROUND HARROGATE- £4.95	
118 SHORT CIRCULAR WALKS IN THE *NORTH YORKS MOORS- £4.95*	
407 NORTH YORKSHIRE MOORS CHALLENGE WALK - £3.95	
602 THE CLEVELAND WAY- £4.95	
352 CYCLING AROUND THE NORTH YORKS MOORS - £4.95	

From-
Name

Address

64